D0991394

TRADITION AND CHANGE IN POSTINDUSTRIAL JAPAN

The Role of the Political Parties

Roger Benjamin
Kan Ori

PRAEGER

PRAEGER SPECIAL STUDIES • PRAEGER SCIENTIFIC

Library of Congress Cataloging in Publication Data

Benjamin, Roger W
    Tradition and change in postindustrial Japan.

    Bibliography: p.
    1. Political parties--Japan. 2. Japan--Politics and
government--1945-   I. Ori, Kan, 1933-   Joint
author.   II. Title.
JQ1698.A1B424   324.252   80-28559
ISBN 0-03-059138-4

Published in 1981 by Praeger Publishers
CBS Educational and Professional Publishing
A Division of CBS, Inc.
521 Fifth Avenue, New York, New York 10175 U.S.A.

Dedicated to our mothers
To: EVELYN L. GRIFFITHS and
in memory of TAZO (TAMAJI) ORI

ACKNOWLEDGMENTS

We have a deep sense of gratitude to two groups that have
made this book possible. First, we would like to acknowledge foundation support, which is so vital to research, especially collabora-
tive comparative work between investigators living and traveling between Tokyo and Minneapolis. Ori was supported by the Matsunaga
Foundation and a Visiting Fulbright Fellowship, which allowed him
to spend a year in the United States at a crucial point in the development of the research project (1970-71). Benjamin was supported by
a Fulbright Research Fellowship, which allowed him to begin his
field work in Japan in 1969-70. The Institute of International Relations, Sophia University, and the University of Tokyo's Institute of
Social Science graciously granted him important institutional affiliation. A single-quarter leave from the University of Minnesota and
a travel research grant from the Office of International Programs,
University of Minnesota, aided the progress of the research greatly
as well. The computer facilities of Sophia University and the University of Minnesota provided grants to allow the data analysis.
Finally, both authors wish to thank the East-West Center Communication facilities, which allowed the authors to consult at an important stage in the project during the summer of 1973.

(over)

Roger Benjamin and Kan Ori, Tradition and Change in Postindustrial
Japan: The Role of the Political Parties (New York: Praeger
Publishers, 1981).

But the second group was the most important element in making the work possible. On both sides of the Pacific, numerous individuals aided the authors in gaining access to groups for research purposes, research assistance, and valuable advice and criticism. We were given encouragement and important criticism of portions of the manuscript by Professor Kinhide Mushakoji, Vice Rector, United Nations University; Professor Takeshi Ishida, Institute of Social Science, University of Tokyo; and Professor Timothy Hennessey, Department of Political Science, University of Rhode Island. We would like to thank especially Professor John E. Turner, Department of Political Science, University of Minnesota, who gave us many invaluable suggestions. We would also like to especially thank Professor William Morris, who co-authored part of Chapter 4.

Stephen Coleman, Department of Political Science, University of Minnesota, gave us advice and aid in the analysis for Chapter 4. Mitchell Joelson aided in the data analysis of Chapter 4.

We would like especially to thank Naruo Okunuki and Masaharu Nakamura, who helped to interview our respondents in Chapter 5, and Masanori Ogushi (graduate students at Sophia University), who assisted in the compilation of data for Chapter 2 and Appendix A. We thank Shannon Hurley for providing effective editorial assistance. We also thank Julie Murphy, who cheerfully typed and retyped more versions of the manuscript than we care to recall.

We have worked out some of our ideas in previous publications: we are grateful to the editors of Quality-Quantity: The European-American Journal of Methodology for permission to reprint some of those points here.*

We would share whatever merit this volume has with the colleagues cited. Naturally, we take responsibility for all errors.

Roger Benjamin
Kan Ori

---

*"A Model of Factions Within the Liberal Democratic Party," Quality-Quantity: The European-American Journal of Methodology 12 (March 1978): 63-74.

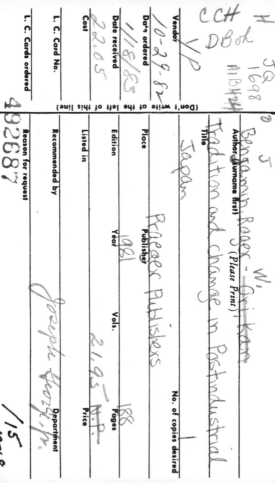

CCH
DBoh
JQ
1698
A1B424

Author (surname first) (*Please Print*)

Benjamin Roger - Chi'rkam

Title Tradition and change in Postindustrial

No. of copies desired   1

Place Japan	**Publisher** Praeger Publishers	
Edition	**Year** 1981	**Vols.** 188
Listed in		**Pages** 21.95 N.P.
		Price

Recommended by Joseph Georgin.

Department

Reason for request

Vendor	V/P
Da'e ordered	10-29-82
Date received	1/18/83
Cost	22.05
L. C. Card No.	
L. C. Cards ordered	492687

/15
10-18

(Don't write at the left of this line)

CONTENTS

1
THE QUESTIONS

It is no longer easy to discern the basic structure of Japanese politics. Until recently, there seemed to be little reason to question the vision of a Japan managed, and rather efficiently, by a tripartite coalition of the public bureaucracy, the political parties, led by the dominant Liberal Democratic Party (LDP), and business. Indeed, as we move into the 1980s, this coalition remains in place; the election of June 1980 even reversed the long decline in voter support for the LDP. Moreover, the Japanese economy is now the second largest in the world, having passed the economy of the Soviet Union. Japanese business has been successful in challenging international competitors in shipbuilding, steel, and the automobile industry, to name only a few examples. In the next decade, the Japanese plan to mount additional challenges to the U.S.-dominated airplane and telecommunication industries. The trains run, on time; the phones work; and the mail is delivered, quickly and efficiently. One must respect arguments that emphasize continuity rather than change. Indeed, there is a case to be made that Japan has much to teach the rest of the world.[1]

There is another view stimulated by recent work on the theme of postindustrialization (sometimes called advanced capitalism). This literature was developed first to describe socioeconomic and political change occurring in Western Europe and North America (minus Mexico). In these societies, observers refer to a growing crisis of the state, as governments rise and fall more quickly, as fiscal limits of public sector expenditures are approached, and as conflict rather than stability appears to be the watchword of the day. "Normal" political participation, such as voting, declines, while "nonnormal" political participation, such as that provided through

1

litigation, strikes, and confrontation tactics, rises. Japan, like her counterparts in Western Europe and North America, is becoming a postindustrial society in the basic sense that the service, and especially the public, sector, is rapidly supplanting the industrial sector as the main engine of the economy. Will Japan, then, avoid the conflict and stress evident in the other postindustrial societies?[2] In Japan, there is evidence that it is not "business as usual." A new prime minister succeeds the old one because of new democratic procedures for voting within the LDP factions. Economic growth appears to be slowing; the LDP vote shares continue to oscillate; political demands and political conflict are rising (symbolized by the Narita Airport confrontation); and the increasing activity and power of local action interest groups (jūmin undō) belies the stereotype of an obedient citizenry, compliant to the wishes of the centralized structure of the political elite. What are we to think? Is the Japanese polity on the brink of a radical transformation? If there is to be such a transformation, what will it look like? Or despite the surface "noise," are the familiar themes used to describe Japanese politics in the past still serviceable?

The political party system is at the heart of either "vision" of Japanese politics. The party system is, for example, embodied in the LDP hegemony and is the "transmission belt" between the elites and mass citizenry, which smoothly translates the elites' decisions to the mass public. Alternatively, it may be that the political party system is in decline, as is thought to be the case in other postindustrial societies, and that this itself may be contributing to the rise of the political conflict scenario.

The adherents of the continuity theme in Japanese politics work with a modified pluralist model of Japanese politics. This familiar model looks at politics as a clash of interest groups, where the Diet and the government as a whole are in the business of aggregating and articulating interests into public policy. Japanese interest groups compete with each other within the policymaking arena defined by government and "win" or "lose" on a provisional basis. Thus, Japanese politics is viewed as a process in which central political institutions—such as the ministries in the public bureaucracy and the political party system—anchor a highly stable and productive social and economic system. A complementary vision of Japanese politics is suggested by the corporate model of politics, developed, so far, with largely Western European applications in mind. Corporatism is characterized by a tripartite system of coordination at the central level of government between government, business, and labor interests. Under this system of mutual accommodation, interest groups are arrayed in large and encompassing vertical systems. We noted that Japan is typically described in the tripartite arrangement of authority between the public bureaucracy, the party system, and business; although no one has applied the corporate label to Japan, it may be the best case for it.[3]

Here, we shall move through three steps. First, we shall introduce the major points associated with postindustrialization. (We will only assert and not show that Japan is a member of the postindustrial group of societies.) In this section, we will also introduce the concept collective goods, a somewhat different approach to politics and the political consequences of postindustrialization. Second, we will assert the rationale for studying the role of political parties in the process of political change. In doing so, we will contrast the role of political parties in the West and Japan. Finally, we shall delimit the particular forces that forge the interaction between Japanese political parties and familiar Japanese cultural practices and outside, foreign imports that we examine in this work.

THE IMPACT OF POSTINDUSTRIALIZATION

A challenge to the pluralist vision of Japanese politics is indeed emerging from the work we shall group under postindustrialization (several other plausible labels are used). Specifically, substantial evidence exists for the view that for at least Western Europe, the United States, and Canada, there is "development" beyond development. Apparent threshold changes in society may be creating disjunctures between the polity and the socioeconomic system. The kinds of public policy issues in these countries may set them apart from other countries.

What is the evidence for yet another provisional benchmark, postindustrialization? First, and foremost, the emphasis in the economies of these countries changes over from industry to service, from a concentration on the production of production goods to the production of consumption, service goods. The public sector is a major or even dominant part of the service sector. In the service sector, emphasis on quality of goods delivered supersedes the previous concern for the quantity of goods produced in the industrial sector. This economic change is reflected in the social system, both at the institutional and individual level. At the institutional level, concern for the quality of educational, health, and welfare services rises; it is no longer a question of, for example, the existence of mass public education, but whether the education delivered to citizens is appropriate. At the individual level, a variety of studies suggest that many citizens—especially the younger and better educated—are no longer concerned only with material and security needs, but are interested in social-psychological concerns that

focus on self-actualization, participation, and equality as well. [4]
This means when these citizens are faced with inflation and specters
of energy scarcity, it becomes more difficult to choose between
(now) competing values; more conflict may result. In the political
arena, public policy issues appear to be more complex than before
because of the emphasis on quality of life issues, and citizens are
also less willing than before to accept decisions that run counter to
their wishes. Not only is "normal" politics declining, but citizen
trust in political institutions appears to be declining as well. Below, we shall present evidence that suggests Japan is a member of
the postindustrial group.

Collective Goods and Postindustrial Society

One of the present authors argues elsewhere that it is indeed
the age of participation versus authority, with rising political demands and conflict; therefore, the redesign of our political institutions is both necessary and inevitable. [5] This argument, summarized
here, supports the conflict/change group. The structure of the
argument links the concept postindustrialization to collective goods
theory, one of the family of political economy theories. The reasons for the redesign thrust have to do with the implications of the
rise in the public sector, the increase of collective goods—goods
with externalities attached to them, which drive citizens into collective action—and the inability of political party systems to continue
to perform the transmission belt role. In Japan, as is the case with
the other postindustrial countries, the rise in the public sector,
plus the changing focus of its activities, is especially important.

As industry loses ground to the public sector, it becomes
more difficult to operate the economy by the standard measures of
productivity, cost, and efficiency. Most human service occupations
are such that actual increases in productivity (as measured by classical economic measures) are sporadic or nonexistent. A welfare
officer probably provides more efficient service (as measured by
the quality of his or her performance) when he or she has fewer
cases to handle. In addition, in the absence of the market mechanism, there are no internal ways to avoid an inexorable rise in
costs, both of wages and materials, which seldom remain constant
or decline. Such conditions, we argue, lead to the need to rede-
fine both the nature of the service sector and the way to measure
the quality of the services rendered. From this perspective, for
example, the rise in public sector strikes are to be expected because
in the public sector, the absence of meaningful comparative performance indicators leaves a group's relative strength in collective

action as the only powerful criterion distinguishing, for example, postal workers from university professors in Japan.

While this stimulates heightened debate, another trend, if we have analyzed it correctly, is leading to changes in the structure and the basic functions of the political party system in Japan. There is a trend toward an increase in numbers and importance of goods recently characterized as collective in nature as occupying a central place in economic and political activity. Although substantial confusion and debate about these goods is reflected in uncertainty over nomenclature and conceptual and empirical meaning, the presence of externalities (spillover effects) attached to the production and/or consumption of a good defines it as a collective good. No one minds being forced to consume positive externalities, but one does mind having to consume negative externalities. Since, because of the nature of their production, private goods are divisible, there is little argument over who is going to bear what proportion of the benefits and costs; the laws of supply and demand dictate the solution. With respect to public goods, it is very likely the case that citizens will be "free riders" (not pay their fair share), since, for example, they will receive the benefits of the production of national defense anyway (thus, the need for taxation is born). In any event, the negative spillover effects (externalities) from the free rider problem us ually do not bear dramatically on other citizens because, for one thing, each citizen pays only a small proportion of his/her taxes for any specific public good. With respect to collective goods, it is the confusion over who is to pay what proportion of the costs and who is going to get what proportion of the benefits that is so vexing. Everyone in the domain of a collective good has to put up with the same level and type of costs from the collective good; everyone in the neighborhood surrounding a factory must bear the similar negative externality of air pollution.

Now, just what comprises collective goods is itself a function of public taste; more specifically, the greater the level of socioeconomic development, the less willing citizens are to internalize the negative externalities of goods once assumed to be private. For example, in 1950, citizens in Kawakami, near Tokyo, ignored the effects of air pollution from the steel plants (thus treating it as a private good); in 1980, pollution is regarded as a collective good (negative externality), and laws are being enacted to regulate plant emissions.[6]

Both positional and collective goods are growing in postindustrial societies, and this gives credence to a predicted rise in associated political conflict. If construction and development of largely centralized socioeconomic and political institutions are the hallmark of the industrial era of Japanese (from roughly the Meiji era

until the late 1960s), efforts to cope with the effects of this development, e.g., human services, and the redesign of these institutions
describe the present and future in Japan as a postindustrial society.
Redesign rather than decentralization is called for because the debate over centralization of governmental institutions is miscast.
It is a question of matching the size of the governmental unit with
the good to be delivered, public or collective, and linking these to
the catchment (community) appropriate for consumption of the good.
Because publics are more diverse and better educated, their wants
are also more diverse. This suggests that equal diversity in the
design of political institutions is required.

The Rationale for Studying Political Parties

The social and economic challenges presented to citizens and
elites in postindustrial societies may be similar, but their responses
may be different, due to the particular rate and sequence of political
change in specific countries. It is often argued that cultural differences account for different political responses to socioeconomic
change. If this point has merit, political parties remain an important place to focus attention because the arena occupied by
parties remains at the heart of the political response to basic system challenges.

Political parties have been described as the central mechanism for elite-mass relationships in industrial states. The relationships are many, but center on interest aggregation and articulation, political leadership recruitment, and the ranking of public
policy problems on the national government's agenda. If basic
societal change is occurring, it should be reflected in the political
party system, which necessarily must bear much of the impact of
the new forces. Western European and U.S. scholars are beginning
to write about the decline of political parties. It is alleged that
voting participation is declining, that alternative routes to recruitment for political leadership usurp old party mechanisms, and that
interest groups increasingly bypass the party system and make
their demands directly on government.

Political parties grew out of man's experience in dealing with
the political impact of industrialization, so perhaps it is reasonable
to expect, at a minimum, basic changes in the functions of political
parties in postindustrial societies. Single-issue interest groups
relate to collective not public goods, as parties do, and it is not
surprising that parties find it difficult to aggregate and articulate
such diverse wants from sophisticated, well-educated publics, who
no longer are so willing to live with less than full achievement of

their goals. The political party system remains very much at the center of the political institutional design in all the societies thus far mentioned and so warrants close attention.

But, then, why study Japanese political parties as a microcosm of political change? Our reason will sound familiar to the student of Japanese politics—Japan is the only major non-Western postindustrial society. If we see that Japanese political and party patterns of change are similar to patterns described in Western Europe and the United States, the case for redesign of political institutions in postindustrial societies is strengthened. However, we take adherents of what might be called the cultural approach to Japanese politics seriously, though ultimately, perhaps, for reasons different than is usually the case. Since Japan's culture remains clearly outside the Western paradigm, the possibility (probability?) remains that the Japanese response to the challenge of the transformation from industrialization to postindustrialization will be distinctive. Equally important is the fact that we really lack basic empirical information about key components of the party system; we need the information if we are to answer the questions raised here.

All this really suggests is that we (1) look at recent political party change in Japan carefully, with an eye to providing an efficient contextual description; and (2) conduct this examination with the broader theoretical searchlight suggested here rather than through the standard pluralist visions of Japanese politics.

POLITICAL PARTIES IN JAPAN

We indicated that the political party system is at the heart of either the stability or conflict and change vision of Japanese politics. Though political parties were introduced from outside, that is, a foreign import brought into Japan in the early part of the Meiji period, the political parties have been the main organizational response to the greatly enlarged elite-mass relationships, which developed as a function of industrialization in Japan just as they have developed everywhere else. Intellectuals excluded from the formal political institutions sought to develop bases of support and began to organize the small middle class groups as political parties that began to emerge during the rapid industrialization program of Meiji Japan (1870-1910). As we move into the 1980s, there are a number of vexing issues—conceptual, evidential, and theoretical in nature—that are really as central today, as Japan moves into the postindustrial phase of sociopolitical changes, as during the pre-World War II period.

The foremost issue concerns the understandings we attach to the concept political party set in the Japanese context. We know already, for instance, that party identification in Western Europe differs substantially from the nature of party identification in the United States. We know that to fully understand Japanese understandings concerning the term political party, one must understand the place of political party within the family of related organizational models used to cope with questions of leadership, decision making, and conflict itself, for example, factions (habatsu), personal support organizations (koenkai), reciprocal rights and obligations (on and giri), and decision making from below (ringeisei). That is, political attitudes and behavior encompassed by the concept Japanese political party may differ from the political behavior and attitudes incorporated under the concept U.S. political party. This issue is labeled the emic/etic paradox by Goodenough.[7] Etic concepts are those dimensions of human activity thought comparable across nations and across cultures. The term automobile factory conjures up organizational routines that are indeed standard everywhere. Emic concepts are embedded in the warp and woof of specific cultures in specific times and places. New ideas and concepts diffuse at an increasing rate into societies around the world as we approach the end of the twentieth century. The inclination is to move toward universal, cross-cultural-grounded understandings of concepts, such as political participation, leadership, health, and so forth. However, we shall see here in this book that this diffusion of ideas and concepts does run up against powerful indigenous cultural forces within Japan itself.

The emic/etic distinction is important for our argument, so let us paraphrase the original example drawn by Goodenough. Goodenough demonstrates that the practices understood as falling under marriage differ from one society to the next.[8] This, again, is because marriage can only be understood completely in terms of how it relates to other features in the particular culture. In the United States, marriage may be defined as a contractual arrangement between, usually, a man and a woman. By contrast, in Japan, marriage remains embedded in a more "traditional" kinship system, where such features as omiya (the arranged introduction of the potential marriage partners) must be included. To grasp the notion of Japanese marriage, we need to study it within its emic, Japanese context and not wrench it out of its cultural fabric and try to compare it to marriage across cultures. Yet many times, it is necessary to make such (etic) comparisons. Diffusion of other meanings of marriage (and by analogy similar concepts) are communicated through international communication networks; this diffusion process affects and confuses the etic-defined understandings previously given.

There is no magic solution to the emic/etic paradox; in the analysis of political party change, we must look at the Japanese case for what it says about the general comparative process of party change, that is, for what the particular Japanese case says about the comparative generalizations developed elsewhere. Equally, we must be alert to commonalities in the Japanese political party change process with other nations. This is to be understood as an iterative process that links, more closely, area and comparative research.

A second problem concerns lack of descriptive knowledge about the Japanese party system. For understandable sociology of knowledge reasons, we remain in the dark about many aspects of the Japanese political party system. The post-World War II party system has been in place less than 35 years. During that period, there has been substantial, even bewildering fluctuation in party vote support; there also have been many mergers between parties and many policy stands taken and reversed. There have been repeated efforts to examine factions, but few data have been accumulated. Only recently have scholars begun to examine intensively political attitudes of citizens, and we have a long way to go before we understand why Japanese citizens do or do not vote and for whom they vote and for what reasons. Moreover, how does the political party system relate, if at all, to factions, personal support organizations, and the other "traditional" organizational models embedded in Japanese personal and public life?

Finally, there are theoretical issues of importance that are only rarely touched upon in studies of Japanese politics. The underlying issue concerns the absence of theories or a theory of sociopolitical change. Perhaps this issue can be best posed with an example that forms another paradox. Stimulated by the early work of Kyogoku and Ike,[9] researchers have corroborated the proposition that the positive relationship between urbanization, social class or education, and voting participation found to hold in the United States is reversed in Japan. Rural voters vote more often than urban voters; the better educated and members of the middle and upper classes vote less than their less well educated and lower class counterparts. What are we to make of this reversal? Without a general theory of the sociopolitical change process, we really do not know how to interpret it. It may indeed be the case that the Japanese are "different"; alternatively, perhaps, the level and nature of political party institutionalization are different in the two societies. Moreover, perhaps the two societies are at different points in the sociopolitical change process.

What is the paradox in all of this? Let us comment briefly on a couple of technical questions. Most studies, whether they are comparative or done within the context of Japan (or any other

society), based on statistically derived relationships, are cross-
sectional (based on one point in time) in nature. In the absence
of theories from which one can make point predictions about the
strength, as well as the direction, of the relationships generated,
one necessarily assumes stability in the relationships being studied.
Surely this assumption is unwarranted when one deals with social
systems; they are highly complex and unstable. The interrelation-
ships of a set of social and political variables may account (describe) for a single process under study and yet be inaccurate in
forecasting either the continued existence of the particular set of
relationships or suggest how that process might change.

     This would seem to argue for a return to a straightforward
description and study of Japanese political questions of the sort
raised above. We take the position, however, that one profits from
setting descriptive work within the context of "theories" of comparative sociopolitical change, no matter how provisional they might
be. There are implicit if not explicit theories behind the scenarios
noted above that led to adherents of either vision to develop their
continuity or change argument. We would hazard the assertion that
all work on modern Japanese politics has reacted to or against the
benchmark provided by industrialization. Evidence exists that
Japan, like her counterparts elsewhere, is moving beyond industrialization; it is time to posit a new provisional benchmark and
reexamine conventional understandings regarding socioeconomic
and political change.

     Political parties, we have noted, were institutions developed
for and during the industrialization period in Japan. How will the
party system, and particular parties within the system, respond to
the changing world outlined above? In order to answer this question, we shall present the analysis of the basic elements of the
party system itself. Before turning to that task, we present our
last theoretical point concerning how cultural variables should be
conceptualized. We may be past the "mysterious Orient" emphasis
on Japanese tradition as the central explanatory feature of political
parties and politics, but how should the particular cultural values
and norms that are relevant to Japanese politics be viewed? Let
us present our argument by distinguishing what we call the two
approaches to the role of cultural norms and values and then suggest
a way to integrate them.

The Exogenous-Endogenous Distinction

     To account for emphasis on group-oriented decision making,
vertically defined relationships, and so forth, cultural explanation

adherents emphasize the unique contextual factors in Japanese society. Essentially, this means that tradition becomes a residual
category into which unaccounted properties of Japanese values and
behavior may be placed. We reject this view, but we also have
problems with the assumptions made by comparativists in the other
camp. Their approach generally adheres to a Japanese version of
the convergence thesis.[10] Convergence adherents assume that
social, economic, and political change is clustered, undirectional,
and, in this case, unilineal. For this group, industrialization—
with its political concomitants, such as mass political participation,
political parties, and bureaucratization—is inevitable. Conversely,
existing political structures and value systems are destined to die
out. Empirically based generalizations about the regularities in
cross-national political analysis are the goals of the comparative
group, and contextual factors (tradition or culture for the area
specialists) are considered to be residual categories, and little or
no attention is given to them. Exogenous forces are thus the sum
total of industrialization, which itself reduces or transforms traditional cultural practices to a homogenous worldwide mean.

Our point is, we hope, straightforward. We must not retreat
from our comparative theory construction goals, but to attain them,
we must "unblack-box" the concept of tradition so that we may
understand the cross-national variation in institutionalized patterns,
which, we believe, are crucial for concept formation and theory-
building efforts. We prefer to specify and ground empirically the
institutionalized models we examine so that we may assess their
validity. Let us define our endogenous terms. We shall view
tradition as simply the institutionalized experience stock that societal members have before them at any given time; this, then,
comprises our end set of behavior and attitudes. The greater the
number and variety of the endogenous images and models that guide
and structure behavior, the greater the possibility that they will
continue to exist in rapid socioeconomic change environments
(modernization)—and the greater the possibility that they will be
used in the integrated or exogenous (foreign) models.

Thus, with Eisenstadt, we view endogenous models as "reser-
voirs" for: (1) the major ways of looking at the basic problems of
social and cultural order and of posing the major questions about
them; (2) the various possible answers to these problems; and
(3) the possibilities of using the different institutional, orientational,
and organizational structures available for the implementation of
different types of solutions or answers to these problems.[11]

These remarks are designed to lay the groundwork for our
treatment of the process of political institutionalization in Japan.
With Friedrich and Huntington, we shall define institutions as

especially well delimited, stable, and enduring patterns of behavior.[12] As these patterns acquire value and become routinized, they become complexes of norms relating to a major aspect of social structure. They furnish the codes that tie patterns of action and organization to social values. The form institutions take is a function of their interaction with their environment. Endogenous institutions are formed out of the social equivalent of the natural selection principle; as institutions develop over time, they become complex, attain autonomy compared to other organizations that perform the same or similar functions, and adapt to changes in their environment or die. In this sense, the concept of endogenous institutions gives precise meaning to the characterization of "tradition as the routinized expression of the symbolic dimensions of human endeavor and of its structural derivatives."[13]

Institutionalization, the development of these structuring "codes" that furnish the guides for behavior, usually occurs over a long period of time. The point, worth stressing because of its importance for the chapters that follow, is that these endogenous institutions will persist in the absence of very strong stimuli from their environment. Far from being helpless, economic, social, and, most importantly, political institutions provide a wide array of survival weapons that their elites use when change agents (usually identified with the modernization or industrialization process) are introduced into a society.

This study should be read as an attempt to sort out evidence concerning the Japanese response to foreign (exogenous) change agents that require adaptation. The Japanese reaction to the change agents should be viewed as a continual process of combination and recombination of politically relevant endogenous and exogenous institutions (see Figure 1.1). The Japanese have a parliamentary system and a legislature, the Diet, yet there is a substantial amount of work which suggests that factions form the core structuring principle around which conflict resolution is handled. There is, and has been, a well-articulated party system in Japan at the national, regional (prefectural), and local levels, yet many observers feel that personal support organizations (koenkai) are more important. In response to the complexities of organization and management presented by socioeconomic change following the Meiji Restoration, the Japanese have developed a full-scale public bureaucracy. The way they have gone about it however appears to cast doubt on the convergence thesis. The public bureaucracy continues to enjoy high support from the mass public—higher perhaps than in most major nation-states. The institutionalized norms and values governing social control and conflict resolution may account for this support.

FIGURE 1.1

Juxtaposition of Exogenous and Endogenous Models in the
Process of Political Institutionalization

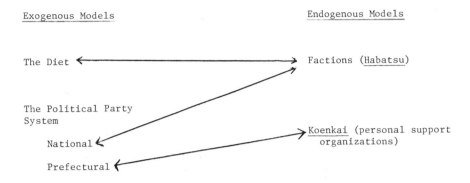

Source: Compiled by the authors.

Plan of Work

　　This book comprises a series of essays (chapters) on the party
system and endogenous features thought to relate to it. The description and assessment of post-World War II political party change is
followed by an examination of the simple question whether and to
what extent the LDP hegemony of the political party system is declining, and if so, by how much. Next, we treat factionalism in
Japanese politics, which many observers think is more important
than the party system. This is followed by an empirical study of
personal support organizations in two prefectural legislatures.
　　We end the study by relating the party system to the overall
process of political change in Japan.

NOTES

　　1. See Edwin Reischauer, Japan: The Japanese (Cambridge,
Mass.: Belknap Press, 1977). Compare Esra F. Vogel, Japan As
Number One: Lessons For America (Cambridge, Mass.: Harvard
University Press, 1979).
　　2. Samuel P. Huntington, "Postindustrial Politics: How
Benign Will It Be?," Comparative Politics 6 (January 1974): 163-91.

Political economists of Marxist and non-Marxist persuasion write about the same problems, but use the advanced capitalism label and, of course, different approaches. See Roger Benjamin, "Minerva and the Crane (Tsuru): Birds of a Feather? Comparative Research and Japanese Political Change," Journal of Asian Studies 40 (November 1980): 69-77.

3. A standard pluralist vision of Japanese politics is contained in Robert E. Ward's Japan's Political System, 2d ed. (Englewood Cliffs, N.J.: Prentice-Hall, 1978). The major corporate statement is by Philippe C. Schmitter, "Still the Century of Corporatism?," in Frederick B. Pike and Thomas Stritch, eds., The New Corporatism (Notre Dame, Ind.: University of Notre Dame Press, 1974), pp. 85-131.

4. Ronald Inglehart, "The Silent Revolution in Europe: Intergenerational Change in Post-Industrial Societies," American Political Science Review 65 (December 1971): 991-1007

5. Roger Benjamin, The Limits of Politics: Collective Goods and Political Change in Postindustrial Societies (Chicago: University of Chicago Press, 1980).

6. Fred Hirsch, The Social Limits to Growth (Cambridge, Mass.: Harvard University Press, 1976).

7. Ward Goodenough, Description and Comparison in Cultural Anthropology (Chicago: Aldine, 1970).

8. Ibid.

9. Junichi Kyogoku and Nobutaka Ike, "Urban-rural Differences in Voting Behavior in Postwar Japan," The Proceedings of the Department of Social Sciences, College of General Education, University of Tokyo, no. 9 (Tokyo: University of Tokyo, 1959).

10. Ian Weinberg, "The Problems of the Convergence of Industrial Societies: A Critical Look at the State of a Theory," Comparative Studies in Society and History 11 (January 1969): 1-15.

11. S. N. Eisenstadt, Tradition, Change, and Modernity (New York: John Wiley and Sons, 1973), p. 337.

12. Carl J. Friedrich, Man and His Government: An Empirical Theory (New York: McGraw-Hill, 1963), p. 70; Huntington, op. cit.

13. Eisenstadt, op. cit., p. 140.

2
ELECTORAL CHANGE AND POLITICAL PARTY SUPPORT BASES

THE POLITICAL PARTY SYSTEM

While this work is concerned with a number of endogenous institutionalized features crucial to understanding the basic elements in Japanese political change, the place to begin is with a review of the political party system.[1] The political party system is exogenous in origin, but has been salient in Japanese politics for a century. We shall concentrate on the postwar period by discussing the patterns of electoral change and mapping organizational dimensions of political parties and their interest group bases.[2] First, though, we need to place the party system in relationship to the Diet, local-national governmental structures, and the public bureaucracy.

The Diet consists (in 1980) of a lower house, the House of Representatives, with 511 members chosen from 130 electoral districts, and the House of Councillors (upper house), comprised of 252 members elected from the 47 prefectures and at large. The House of Representatives is the more important body because it may override a negative vote in the House of Councillors by passing the bill again by a two-thirds vote. Even this is not necessary for treaties and budgets opposed by the upper house if the lower house passes the bill at least one month prior to the legislative session's end. While members of the House of Representatives are elected for maximum terms of four years, the members of the House of Councillors serve for six years; this provides greater continuity, since only one-half of the members stand for election every three years. Each voter casts one vote for a House of Councillor prefectural candidate and one other vote for a House of Councillor candidate at large. Each district of the House of Representatives has from three to five representatives (with one exception, Amami, which is a single-member district). Except in 1946, the postwar elections for the House of Representatives have been held under this variation of the multiple-member district system.*

Japan, like France, Great Britain, and Italy, is a unitary system; whereas all roads lead to Rome in Italy, in Japan, all roads lead to Nihonbashi Bridge in Tokyo. This is reflected in the relationships between the national, prefectural, and local levels of

---

*The "large-size electoral district" arrangement used in the 1946 election had the following characteristics. Election districts were usually prefecture-at-large, with the exception of seven larger prefectures (such as Tokyo, Osaka, Hokkaido, and so forth), which contained two electoral districts. Depending on the population size, these districts elected from four to 14 members to the House of Representatives. This is also the plural ballot system (limited plural listing, to be precise) in which (1) if a district elects less than five members to the House of Representatives, in that district, a voter has only one vote (that is, only one candidate's name can be listed); (2) in those districts where five to ten members of the House are elected, the voter may cast as many as two votes (if he/she decides to cast only one ballot, that is all right, that is, listing only one name); and (3) in those districts electing more than 11 members to the House, the voter there can cast up to three votes (that is, three names of the candidates can be put on the ballot). The candidates are elected by plurality (in a ten-man district, the top ten men are winners), provided that they fulfill the legally required number of votes (and in this particular election, two in fact did not make it, and a reelection was held).

The first postwar elections for the House of Representatives were held in April 1946. This election should be considered abnormal for several reasons. First, it was held in the immediate aftermath of the war, with accompanying confusion and chaos. Second, reflecting the confusion of the period, there were many independents and minor parties, which makes systematic analysis difficult. Third, this election was conducted under the "large" electoral district arrangement, rather than the "medium-size" one that has been in operation since. For these reasons, the election of 1946 is excluded in our discussion. Since 1947, Japan has had 13 general elections for the House of Representatives, the last of which was held in October 1979.

In the prewar days, Japan had a variety of electoral district systems, ranging from a single-member to medium-size to large electoral district arrangements.

politics. In addition to an assembly where the same parties that exist at the national level compete, each of the 47 prefectures, including Okinawa, is headed by a governor. Village, town, and city assemblies and mayors complete the lower level of political structures. Governors and mayors are clearly the most important ingredients at the regional and local levels of politics, but neither looms especially large in an overall system that allows only one-third of the budget to be allocated, and thus controlled, by them.

These structural relationships are set within the framework of a Constitution written by Allied Occupation authorities in 1946 and inaugurated by the Japanese government in 1947. The current Constitution emphasizes liberal democratic values. The Constitution provides for popular sovereignty (the previous Meiji Constitution of 1888 delegated sovereignty to the emperor), specifies a standard list of civil liberties (Chapter III of the Constitution), stipulates relationships between the Diet and the Cabinet (Chapters IV and V), and contains constitutional amendment and referendum procedures (Chapter IX). The controversial Article 9 of Chapter II contains the clause in which "the Japanese people forever renounce war as a sovereign right of the nation and the threat or use of war as a means of settling international disputes" and which affirms "land, sea, and air forces, as well as other war potential, will never be maintained."

The cabinet is composed of the prime minister, the head of government, who in turn appoints his ministers of state. Although the Constitution states that only a majority of the ministers must be members of the Diet, few non-Diet members have been appointed cabinet members. Typically, there is much cabinet shuffling by the prime minister, who is elected for two-year terms as party president and constantly attempts to maximize strength by rearranging reward incentives for party leaders (heads of factions). Formally, the prime minister is elected by the entire Diet, but in practice, the leader of the majority party—the LDP since 1955—is automatically elected.

Since cabinet ministers come and go, the administrative vice-ministers and other permanent, and important, members of the ministry control a great deal of information and power.

Unlike membership in the U.S. Congress, the total number of seats in the House of Representatives is not fixed. The number of seats has fluctuated from 466 to 511 in the postwar period, as the number of electoral districts increased from 117 to 130, and some urban districts gained seats due to the increase in their population. *

---

*From 1946 to 1955, Japan had 117 electoral districts, with 466 seats; in 1955, the House seats were increased to 467, with an

The present (1980) membership of the House of Representatives is 511, covering 47 prefectures, which includes Okinawa, returned to Japan in 1972.

In electing members of the lower house, each Japanese voter casts only one ballot, despite the fact that each electoral district has three to five representatives. If, for example, nine candidates run for four seats, the top four vote-getters are declared winners. The voters in Japan must also write in the name of a candidate of their choice. The voting act itself does not present a serious problem, but it does suggest significant long-run political consequences for the process of party identification. Writing in an individual candidate's name does not reinforce the party identification and party ticket voter concept, for example, there is nothing comparable to the U.S. straight party ticket voting in Japan. This encourages individual- rather than party-based voting.* In fact, what is characterized as the party vote is nothing but the sum of all the votes various individual candidates of a given party garnered in that electoral district. For instance, the LDP figure is a total of all the votes the LDP candidates received in that district. This kind of electoral arrangement is not likely to facilitate political party development.

The present electoral system favors minor parties. Larger parties, like the LDP (conservatives) and the Japan Socialist Party are clearly handicapped, since it is very difficult for them to arrive at an optimal number of candidates in a given district where they can afford to put up plural candidates (and this is almost always the case for the LDP). Furthermore, even if they could decide on the optimal number of candidates, it is very difficult for them to distribute their votes optimally among several candidates. It is not impossible for them to lose two seats with three candidates simply because one popular candidate happens to get an unnecessarily high number of votes, whereas if they could apportion their total votes more or less

---

addition of one more district (N = 118). In 1967, the electoral district system was changed to 123 districts, which lasted until 1972 (with 486 seats), at which time Okinawa was returned, thus adding five representatives and one more district. Since 1976, there have been 130 electoral districts, with 511 seats.

*As to the bases of voting (individual factors versus party) note, for example, in late 1972, 46 percent of the Japanese electorate voted on the basis of the individual and 33 percent for the party (cannot say either way, 20 percent; others and don't know, 1 percent) (the Mainichi Shimbun survey of November 10-12, 1972, reported in the same paper on November 24, 1972).

equally among three candidates, they would win all three seats. On the other hand, minor parties can concentrate on maximizing their votes, because ordinarily, they put up only one candidate per district.

Each prefecture has its own assembly. The assembly size differs, depending on the population base, ranging from around 40 members in rural prefectures to over 100 in urban prefectures. Prefectural assemblymen are ordinarily elected every four years, unless there are vacancies due to sudden death, resignation, or dissolution of the assembly by recall. The first general prefectural assembly elections were held in 1947, and the last such elections were conducted in 1979. Election districts for the prefectural assemblies vary from a single-member to a large-size (18-member) district. Whereas prefectural governors were appointed in prewar days by the Ministry of Interior, since 1947, they have been elected at large.

Finally, at the local level, town or village assemblies consisting of as few as five members and metropolitan assemblies of more than 100 are elected.

There are many independent candidates in both prefectural and local assembly elections. Independents also compete in some of the metropolitan mayoral and prefectural governors' races. Generally, the highest percentage of independents is evident at the local assemblies, the next at the prefectural level; few are found at the national level elections. However, in recent years, independents have been decreasing in number at the prefectural assembly level as well.

ELECTORAL PARTICIPATION

The voting participation rate of the postwar era is shown in Table 2.1; it ranges from 68 percent to 77 percent for the House of Representatives' elections. In comparison, the voter turnout rate in prewar days was considerably higher, almost 90 percent before 1925, when the Japanese electorate was quadrupled due to the introduction of universal male suffrage. Even after 1925, it remained above the 80 percent level in four out of six elections. Two points stand out with respect to voter participation. First, Tables 2.1 and 2.2 demonstrate that the higher the election level, the lower the voter turnout. Voting is highest in local elections and lowest in national elections. This is the reverse of the U.S. pattern, but similar to the French case. Also note that a sharper decline takes place between the prefectural and local levels than between the national and prefectural elections. Second, there are distinct urban-

differences in voting participation. Tables 2.3 and 2.4 give voter turnout rates for the House of Representatives and prefectural assembly elections in selected urban and rural prefectures for the entire postwar period. The urban prefectures have much lower levels of voter participation than rural prefectures for both types of elections. We will examine this phenomenon in greater detail in Chapter 3.

TABLE 2.1

Voter Participation for the House of Representatives
Elections, 1946-80

Election Year	Number of Eligible Voters (N)	Voter Participation Rate (percent)
1946	36,878,420	72.08
1947	40,907,493	67.95
1949	42,105,300	74.04
1952	46,772,584	76.43
1953	47,090,167	74.22
1955	49,235,375	75.84
1958	52,013,529	76.99
1960	54,312,993	73.51
1963	58,281,678	71.14
1967	62,992,796	73.99
1969	69,260,424	68.51
1972	73,769,636	71.76
1976	79,926,588	73.45
1979	80,169,924	68.01
1980	81,266,330	74.57

Sources: Jichisho senkyobu (Election Bureau, Ministry of Local Autonomy), Shugiin giin sosenkyo kekkashirabe [Results of general elections for the House of Representatives] (1970); Shugiin jimukyoku (House of Representatives Secretariat, Shugiin giin sosenkyo ichiran [A report on the general elections for the House of Representatives] (1973); Jichisho senkyobu (Election Bureau, Ministry of Local Autonomy), Shugiin giin sosenkyo kekkashirabe [Results of general elections for the House of Representatives] (Sokuho) (1977); Asahi shimbun (Asahi newspaper), October 9, 1979, and Asahi shimbun, June 28, 1980.

TABLE 2.2

Voter Participation Rate for Prefectural and Local Assembly Elections, 1947–79
(in percent)

Election Year	Prefectural Assembly	Nine Big Cities	Local Assembly Other Cities	Towns and Villages
1947	81.65	—	—	—
1951	82.99	72.92	90.56	95.92
1955	77.24	62.26	85.00	92.33
1959	79.48	65.09	85.81	92.50
1963	76.85	65.60	82.32	91.50
1967	71.31	57.65	77.90	91.53
1971	72.93	59.87	78.18	92.43
1975	73.94	64.43	77.59	92.67
1979	69.24	57.80	76.09	92.37

Sources: Jichisho senkyobu (Election Bureau, Ministry of Local Autonomy), Toitsu chihosenkyo kekkashirabe [Results of unified local elections] (1971); Jichisho senkyobu (Election Bureau, Ministry of Local Autonomy), Chihosenkyo kekkashirabe (1975); and Jichisho senkyobu (Election Bureau, Ministry of Local Autonomy), Toitsu chihosenkayo kekka no gaiyo [Summary of the results of unified local elections] (Sokuho [Express report]) (1979).

TABLE 2.3

Voter Turnout Rates for the House of Representatives Elections in Selected Urban and Rural Prefectures, 1946–79
(in percent)

Prefectures	1946	1947	1949	1952	1953	1955	1958	1960	1963	1967	1969	1972	1976	1979
Urban Prefectures														
Tokyo	66.45	60.38	61.79	62.23	61.89	66.35	69.74	63.42	60.06	64.23	56.35	62.23	64.55	53.19
Kanagawa	67.66	63.66	68.46	69.86	64.94	69.14	60.93	64.04	58.50	67.25	58.21	63.14	68.30	54.71
Aichi	80.83	78.70	82.86	76.83	73.48	75.11	79.69	72.93	67.99	68.69	65.20	67.29	68.78	65.57
Osaka	68.58	65.89	72.87	62.08	60.02	67.13	64.75	62.96	60.45	68.39	58.29	61.49	64.05	60.82
Hyogo	68.38	68.78	71.84	74.89	69.18	70.66	72.17	68.82	66.35	68.55	64.03	64.15	69.76	65.14
Rural Prefectures														
Fukushima	73.01	66.57	73.57	83.69	83.37	83.59	86.39	84.02	82.34	82.81	81.15	83.50	77.75	75.50
Nagano	72.91	70.95	81.66	85.84	84.13	86.64	86.92	83.45	81.96	83.99	81.49	82.66	83.72	78.09
Shimane	78.81	76.86	90.16	87.91	86.42	87.25	85.61	86.51	85.11	86.87	83.31	86.88	87.88	85.24
Tottori	75.49	72.40	80.82	87.15	83.69	83.32	83.13	80.32	80.91	80.86	81.88	84.21	87.87	83.58
Kochi	74.24	72.10	75.90	77.51	74.04	72.68	79.57	76.01	74.83	82.03	79.61	80.44	78.30	74.77
All Japan	71.94	67.77	74.05	76.43	74.22	75.84	76.99	73.50	71.14	73.99	68.51	71.76	73.45	68.01

Sources: Shugiin jimukyoku (House of Representatives Secretariat), Shugiin giin sosenkyo ichiran [A report on the general elections for the House of Representatives] (Tokyo: Government Printing Office, 1973); Jichisho senkyobu (Election Bureau, Ministry of Local Autonomy), Shugiin giin sosenkyo kekkashirabe [Results of general elections for the House of Representatives] (Sokuho [Express report] (1977); Asahi shimbun [Asahi newspaper], October 9, 1979.

TABLE 2.4

Voter Turnout Rates for the Prefectural Assembly Elections in Selected Urban and Rural Prefectures, 1947–79
(in percent)

Prefectures	1947	1951	1955	1959	1963	1967	1971	1975	1979
Urban Prefectures									
Tokyo	63.2	65.0	59.63	70.13	67.85	58.58(1965)*	59.73(1969)*	66.46	52.55
Kanagawa	75.9	71.0	63.66	72.58	66.51	61.89	65.79	67.67	54.77
Aichi	84.3	82.4	75.39	74.69	68.41	57.90	62.41	64.28	57.91
Osaka	70.3	73.5	63.28	71.07	70.23	56.37	63.23	66.27	63.31
Hyogo	79.4	78.0	70.61	71.26	67.12	58.38	60.36	62.00	52.70
Rural Prefectures									
Fukishima	86.4	90.5	85.85	85.90	87.16	83.77	84.58	84.20	80.05
Nagano	85.9	91.8	85.98	87.01	84.49	81.01	84.10	85.35	81.34
Shimane	87.4	95.1	87.71	89.93	89.36	83.83	89.52	90.61	86.64
Tottori	88.3	92.2	87.70	86.62	81.52	83.88	84.86	84.64	79.07
Kochi	82.2	87.0	79.09	81.51	81.98	77.98	78.18	75.94	69.86
All Japan	81.6	83.0	77.24	79.48	76.85	71.31	72.93	73.94	69.24

*Voter turnout rates for the supplementary elections of Tokyo held in 1967 and 1971 were 66.41 percent and 71.20 percent, respectively.

Sources: Jichisho senkyobu (Election Bureau, Ministry of Local Autonomy), Chihosenkyo kekkashirabe (1951-75); Naimusho chihokyoku (Local Bureau, Ministry of Home Affairs), Showu 22 nen 4 gatsu shikko shugiingiin, sangiingiin, todufuken-chiji, shikuchoson-cho, chihōgikaigiin sōsenkyo kekkashirabe [Results of general elections for the House of Representatives, House of Councillors, Prefectural Governors, City, Ward, Town and Village Mayors and Local Assemblies held in April 1947] (Tokyo: Ministry of Home Affairs, 1947]; Jichisho senkyobu (Election Bureau, Ministry of Local Autonomy), Toitsu chihosenkyo kekka no taiyo (Sokuho) [Summary of original election results (report)], 1979.

23

Why do rates of voting participation vary by level of election and by level of urbanization? Various scholars have attempted to answer this question as it concerns Japan; their answers can be broadly grouped into two categories. First, the lower the level of the election and/or the more rural the constituency, the more immediate political concern becomes accounting for the higher rate of participation. Second, the lower the level of election is and/or the more rural the area becomes, the more voters are mobilized by buraku ("hamlet") solidarity, and this results in the higher rate of participation.[3]

PARTY SUPPORT PATTERN, 1947-79

There are six major political parties in Japan. The dominant conservative Liberal Democratic Party has been in existence since 1955. The LDP is the result of a merger between the Liberal and Democratic parties in reaction to a union of their Socialist competitors. The second and major opposition party is the Japan Socialist Party. The Democratic Socialist Party, which splintered from the Japan Socialist Party in 1960, and the Japan Communist Party are the other "left" parties. Komeito entered the political arena of the House of Representatives for the first time in 1967 and is sponsored by Sokagakkai, the Nichiren-shoshu sect of Japanese Buddhism. The New Liberal Club was born in 1976 as a splinter movement from the LDP.

Various parties (see Figure 2.1) were founded in the postwar era, but we may group them into three categories. First is the conservative bloc, which consists of the Liberal, Progressive, and Cooperative parties. Two major conservative parties are, of course, the Liberal Party (to be more precise, the Japan Liberal Party, Democratic-Liberal Party, and Liberal Party) and the Progressive Party (the Japan Progressive Party, Japan Democratic Party, People's Democratic Party, and Progressive Party). Both of them can trace back their origin to the prewar days, the predecessor of the Liberal Party being the Seiyukai and that of the Progressive Party, the Minseito. They merged in November 1955 to form the present LDP, and the New Liberal Club splintered from the LDP in 1976. The Japan Cooperative Party (a special brand of conservatives) was absorbed by the Progressive Party in 1950.

The Socialist parties constitute the second category. The Japan Socialist Party was formed in November 1945 as an amalgamation of three major proletariat movements of the prewar era. The party then split between the right and left wings, eventually forming two separate parties with the same name (that is, the Japan Socialist

FIGURE 2.1

Postwar Japanese Political Parties, 1950-80

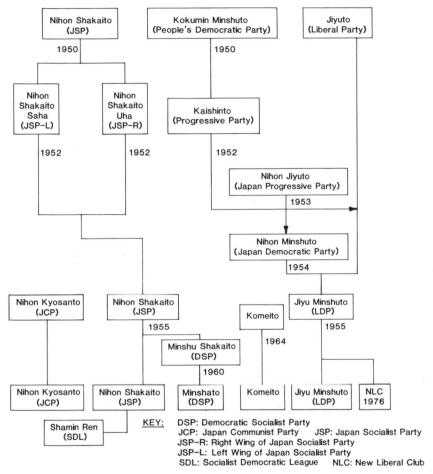

KEY: DSP: Democratic Socialist Party
JCP: Japan Communist Party   JSP: Japan Socialist Party
JSP-R: Right Wing of Japan Socialist Party
JSP-L: Left Wing of Japan Socialist Party
SDL: Socialist Democratic League   NLC: New Liberal Club

Sources: Adapted from Asahi shimbun [Asahi newspaper] and Asahi nenkan [Asahi yearbook] (Tokyo: Asahi Shimbunsha, 1978).

Party Right and the Japan Socialist Party Left) in 1952; they were finally reunited in October 1955. As already mentioned, the Democratic Socialist Party splintered from the party in January 1960; another splinter group from the Japan Socialist Party formed the Socialist Democratic League in 1978. Third, there are two distinct minor parties. One is the Japan Communist Party, and the other is Komeito.

We begin our discussion of electoral trends in party support by looking at the period 1947 to 1967. Table 2.5 indicates that the most

TABLE 2.5

Results of Postwar General Elections for the House of Representatives, 1947–80

Percentage of House Seats

Elections	LDP[a]	New Liberal Club	JSP[b]	Democratic Socialist Party	Japan Communist Party	Komeito	Minor Parties	Independents
1947	60.3	n.a.[c]	30.7	n.a.	0.8	n.a.	5.4	2.8
1949	74.5	n.a.	10.3	n.a.	7.5	n.a.	5.1	2.6
1952	69.6	n.a.	23.8	n.a.	—	n.a.	2.4	4.1
1953	66.5	n.a.	29.6	n.a.	0.2	n.a.	1.3	2.4
1955	63.6	n.a.	33.4	n.a.	0.4	n.a.	1.3	1.3
1958	61.5	n.a.	35.5	n.a.	0.2	n.a.	0.2	2.6
1960	63.4	n.a.	31.0	3.7	0.6	n.a.	0.2	1.1
1963	60.6	n.a.	30.8	4.9	1.1	n.a.	—	2.6
1967	57.0	n.a.	28.8	6.2	1.0	5.1	—	1.9
1969	59.2	n.a.	18.5	6.4	2.9	9.7	0.4	3.3
1972	55.2	n.a.	24.0	3.9	7.7	5.9	—	2.9
1976	48.7	3.3	24.1	5.7	3.3	10.8	—	4.1
1979	48.5	0.8	20.9	6.9	7.6	11.1	0.4	3.7
1980	55.6	2.3	20.9	6.3	5.7	6.5	0.6	2.2
N =	(284)	(12)	(107)	(32)	(29)	(33)	(3)	(11)

Percentage of Popular Votes

Year								
1947	58.90	n.a.	26.20	n.a.	3.70	n.a.	5.40	5.80
1949	63.00	n.a.	13.50	n.a.	9.70	n.a.	7.20	6.60
1952	66.10	n.a.	21.20	n.a.	2.60	n.a.	3.40	6.70
1953	65.70	n.a.	26.60	n.a.	1.90	n.a.	1.40	4.40
1955	63.20	n.a.	29.20	n.a.	2.00	n.a.	2.30	3.30
1958	57.80	n.a.	32.90	n.a.	2.60	n.a.	0.70	6.00
1960	57.56	n.a.	27.56	8.77	2.93	n.a.	0.35	2.83
1963	54.67	n.a.	29.03	7.37	4.01	n.a.	0.15	4.77
1967	48.80	n.a.	27.89	7.40	4.76	5.38	0.22	5.55
1969	47.63	n.a.	21.44	7.74	6.81	10.91	0.17	5.30
1972	46.85	n.a.	21.90	6.98	10.49	8.46	0.27	5.05
1976	41.78	4.18	20.69	6.28	10.38	10.91	0.08	5.70
1979	44.60	3.00	19.70	6.80	10.40	9.80	0.80	4.90
1980	47.90	3.00	19.30	6.60	9.80	9.00	0.90	3.50

[a] From 1947 to 1955 inclusive, LDP stands for all the major conservative parties; since the 1958 election, it means the Liberal Democratic Party.

[b] From 1947 to 1955 inclusive, JSP stands for all the Socialist parties except the Laborer Farmer Party, which is counted as a minor party; since the 1958 election, it means the Japan Socialist Party.

[c] Not applicable.

Sources: Adapted from Jichisho senkyobu (Election Bureau, Ministry of Local Autonomy), Shugiin giin sosenkyo kekkashirabe [Results of general elections for the House of Representatives] (1973); Jichisho senkyobu (Election Bureau, Ministry of Local Autonomy), Shugiin ginn sosenkyo kekkashirabe [Results of general elections for the House of Representatives] (1977); and Asahi shimbun [Asahi newspaper], October 9, 1979.

salient fact about the electoral record for this period (1947-63) is
the continuous dominance of the conservatives. From 1947 to 1967,
the conservative bloc maintained a comfortable majority of between
54. 7 percent and 66. 1 percent of the popular vote and more than 60
percent of the House seats.*

During the same period, the combined Socialist forces did not
range above 36. 5 percent of the vote in elections for the House of
Representatives (see Table 2. 5). The Socialist Party (JSP), itself,
has not exceeded 33 percent of the total popular vote in national
elections or 36 percent of the House of Representatives. Also, if
the election of 1949 is excluded, minor parties have been insignifi-
cant, especially since the 1955 merger of parties.

The 1967 general election for the House of Representatives is
significant because it apparently marks the beginning of a new trend
toward a multiparty pattern in Japan, at least in the opposition camp.
In this election, the LDP fell below its consistent majority in popular support for the first time since its establishment in 1955 and
elected only 277 members to the House (about 57 percent of its total
membership). The Socialist Party did not, however, gain propor-
tionately to the LDP loss; indeed, its percentage of House seats declined from that of the previous election, marking the lowest point
hitherto in its popularity since its consolidation in 1955. While the
LDP and the Socialist Party were thus losing, the Democratic Socialist Party, Komeito, and the Communist Party all increased their
strength in the 1967 election for the House of Representatives. This
development has been described by Japanese political analysts as
"the Tatoka phenomenon," that is, the growth of two or more opposition parties with significant political strength in contrast to the former situation, when only one opposition party with significant political strength challenged the ruling party.

Basically a tendency toward multipartization, the Tatoka phenomenon began in the 1960s in local urban centers. In the Osaka
municipal election of 1963, for instance, the LDP captured 40 seats,

---

*It is to be noted, however, that for a brief period in 1947-48,
Japan had a Socialist-led coalition government. In the 1947 election, the Japan Socialist Party became the plurality party. Some
scholars divide the postwar period differently than we do, by label-
ing the period from 1946 to 1955 as a multiparty era and from 1955
on as a dominant one-party system, but we feel our periodization is
better fitted for the analysis presented here. The 1946 election is
excluded for our discussion because it was held under a different
electoral district arrangement.

while the Democratic Socialist Party won 18; the Socialist Party, 12; Komeito, eight; the Communist Party, five; and independents, two. Similarly, after the 1963 election, the Kyoto City Assembly had the following distribution of seats: the LDP, 24; the Socialist Party, 13; the Democratic Socialist Party, eight; the Communist Party, eight; Komeito, seven; and independents, eight. The distribution of seats for the Kobe Municipal Assembly after the 1963 election was as follows: the LDP, 31; the Socialist Party, 16; the Democratic Socialist Party, eight; Komeito, six; the Communist Party, one; and independents, six. Even taking into account a scandal involving LDP members, the 1965 Tokyo Metropolitan Assembly election result is fascinating; the Socialist Party, which became the first party, won 45 seats; the Liberal Democratic Party, 38; Komeito, 23; the Communist Party, nine; the Democratic Socialist Party, four; and independents, one.

Table 2.6, which contains data concerning the 1965 House of Councillors elections, shows a similar trend toward the multiparty pattern in urban areas. In the city of Tokyo proper, for example, only 21.8 percent of the voters supported the LDP "local constituency" candidates for the upper house, whereas 17.3 percent supported the Socialist Party, 16.2 percent, Komeito, and 16.1 percent, the Communist Party. The situation was somewhat similar in Kobe: the Socialist Party candidates received 30.2 percent of the popular vote; the LDP, 23.7 percent; Komeito, 21.8 percent; and the Democratic Socialist Party, 17.4 percent.

In the urban settings in the 1960s, the multiparty trend was also noticeable in the House of Representatives elections. Table 2.7 indicates the percentage distribution of votes in five cities in 1963 and 1967. In Osaka, the Tatoka phenomenon was manifested as early as 1963; while the LDP received 37.4 percent of the votes, other parties, such as the Socialist Party, the Democratic Socialist Party, and the Communist Party, received approximately 20 percent each. Table 2.7 also makes it clear that in metropolitan areas, the LDP has already become a party of only one-third of the electorate. The status of the Socialist Party shows a similar pattern of decline. While in comparison with 1963, it only lost 1.1 percent of the nationwide popular vote in 1967, its loss in the cities was most remarkable: 9.2 percent in Tokyo, for instance, and 13.2 percent in Kobe. A similar though less dramatic dispersion of party strength in urban areas is observable in Table 2.8, which contains election results for the House of Representatives in 36 urban election districts and 17 rural election districts of the nation throughout the 1960s.

TABLE 2.6

Results of the 1965 Election for the House of Councillors
(Local Constituency) in Seven Metropolitan Cities
(percent)

Cities	Liberal Democratic Party	Japan Socialist Party	Komeito	Democratic Socialist Party	Japan Communist Party	Minor Parties and Independents	Total
Tokyo	21.8	17.3	16.2	9.9	16.1	18.7	100.0
Yokohama	29.8	35.9	—	18.5	6.3	9.5	100.0
Nagoya	29.9	30.0	20.7	10.7	7.2	1.5	100.0
Kyoto	30.3	28.4	—	18.4	22.9	—	100.0
Osaka	29.0	16.0	22.9	18.9	10.9	2.5	100.0
Kobe	23.7	30.2	21.8	17.4	6.9	—	100.0
Kitakyushu	36.6	32.3	15.2	5.1	10.8	—	100.0
All Japan (local constituency)	44.2	32.8	5.1	6.1	6.9	4.9	100.0

Source: Sangiin jimukyoku (House of Councillors Secretariat), Sangiin giin senkyo ichiran (Tokyo: Government Printing Office, 1965).

TABLE 2.7

Results of the 1963 and 1967 Elections for the House of Representatives
(percent)

Constituency	Years	Liberal Democratic Party	Komeito	Democratic Socialist Party	Japan Socialist Party	Japan Communist Party	Others
All Japan	1963	54.7	—	7.4	29.0	4.0	4.9
	1967	48.8	5.4	7.4	27.9	4.8	5.7
Tokyo	1963	44.1	—	10.2	36.3	6.9	2.5
	1967	32.1	13.1	11.8	27.1	9.9	6.0
Kyoto	1963	40.3	—	14.7	27.8	16.7	4.9
	1967	31.9	10.0	12.7	24.4	16.3	4.7
Osaka	1963	37.4	—	19.9	21.4	19.5	1.7
	1967	24.0	20.0	19.6	17.6	11.0	7.9
Kobe	1963	37.5	—	11.6	44.6	5.4	0.9
	1967	27.0	19.2	12.1	31.4	6.6	3.7
Kitakyushu	1963	33.5	—	16.5	37.7	9.0	0.3
	1967	29.3	8.5	16.2	32.3	12.1	1.6

Source: Shugiin jimukyoku (House of Representatives Secretariat), Shugiin giin sosenkyo ichiran [A report on the general elections for the House of Representatives] (Tokyo: Office of Prime Minister, 1963, 1967).

TABLE 2.8

Results of General Elections for the House of Representatives in the
36 Urban Election Districts and 17 Rural Election Districts
(percent)

Years	Liberal Democratic Party	Japan Socialist Party	Democratic Socialist Party	Japan Communist Party	Komeito	Minor Parties and Independents
			Urban-Type Election Districts			
1960	50.4	30.8	12.1	4.8	—	1.9
1963	46.5	32.0	12.5	6.5	—	2.5
1967	36.4	27.2	11.8	7.4	12.1	5.1
			Rural-Type Election Districts			
1960	66.5	21.0	6.2	1.6	—	4.7
1963	62.0	24.3	3.2	2.2	—	8.3
1967	74.7	26.8	1.1	2.5	1.3	3.6

Source: Editorial Staff, "DAISANSEIRYOKU SHINSHUTSU NO IMI," Asahi janaru [Asahi journal], February 12, 1967, p. 19.

The five elections following the 1967 House of Representatives election suggest the continuation of the Tatoka pattern. Although the LDP still retains a majority in the House of Representatives by recruiting independents after the elections, its strength has continued to decline. The Conservative Party fell below 50 percent majority of the popular vote for the first time in 1967, and its popular support continued to decline to the 1976 election, at which time the party's popularity reached its all-time low of 41.8 percent. Support for the LDP rose to 44.6 percent in the 1979 election. The five elections following the 1967 House of Representatives election suggest the continuation of the Tatoka pattern. Although the LDP now retains a majority of seats in the House of Representatives, its strength continues to fluctuate. For instance, the Conservative Party fell below 50 percent majority of the popular vote for the first time in 1967, and its popular support continued to decline to the 1976 election, at which time the party's popularity fell to 41.8 percent. Support for the LDP rose to 44.6 percent in the 1979 election. Support for opposition parties also oscillated over this same period.

The House of Representatives election of June 22, 1980, presents us with an opportunity to assess the Tatoka phenomena as we move into the 1980s. The Tatoka trend does appear to be continuing (Table 2.5), despite the fact that the LDP made a remarkable comeback, both in terms of House seats and its share of the popular vote. The Japan Socialist Party remained at about the same low level in the 1980 election, in terms of percentage of the popular vote and proportion of seats held in the House of Representatives. However, the two stars of the Tatoka era, Komeito and the Japan Communist Party, lost seats in the House of Representatives, and their shares of the popular vote declined somewhat. Indeed, only the LDP increased its share of the popular vote; the other parties remained constant or declined.

Why did the LDP increase its share of seats and votes? We think the main factor was the higher voter turnout in the June 1980 election. In turn, voter turnout increased in small part because of the fact that the upper House of Councillors election was held at the same time as the lower House election. In larger part, the death of Prime Minister Ohira, in late May, stimulated a greater voter turnout. Greater numbers of independents (no party identification) also voted in this election, and they tended to support the LDP. Higher voter turnout itself detracted from the more well organized parties, Komeito and the Japan Communist Party, because they were not able to add sufficient votes on top of their existing base. In fact, in some cases, as with Komeito, candidates were not able to win seats they held even though their votes increased from the previous election. This is due to the fact that the number of votes went up in the 1980 election as a function of the increased voter turnout.

The 1980 election also showed the resilience of the LDP (see Chapter 3). It should be also noted that many of the runners-up in the election were minor party candidates, and they might make a comeback if the voter turnout again declines in succeeding elections.

ORGANIZATIONAL BASES OF JAPANESE POLITICAL PARTIES

One of the outstanding characteristics of Japanese political parties is their organizational fragility. "None of the parties—save perhaps the Fair Play Party (Komeito)—are truly mass membership organizations."[4] Even Komeito's organizational structure is not a distinct party structure, but is the outgrowth of Sokkagakkai, the religious organization that supports it. Japanese parties lack not only a mass base in terms of membership, but also mass involvement in party affairs at grass-roots level. Because of their campaign for mass public membership, the LDP currently (1980) has about 3 million members, but this figure is attributable to factional considerations. Since 1978, the LDP has held presidential primaries in which all members of the party may vote for their choice for leadership of the LDP. It is now in the interest of all the factions within the LDP to increase their membership base. The Socialist Party, which has been supported by approximately one-third of the electorate throughout most of the postwar period, has a very small membership: it reported only 37,000 persons as of December 31, 1973. At present (1980), the party claims to have approximately 53,000 members, but the 1973 figure is perhaps closer to reality. Recently, under Asukata's leadership, the Japan Socialist Party has also attempted to enlarge its mass base, but without too much success. As of December 1978, Komeito and the Japan Communist Party claimed 142,000 and 400,000 members, respectively, while the Democratic Socialist Party reported 40,000 members.

Japanese parties are primarily parliamentary organizations composed of national professional politicians, their co-workers, and very little else. For most of them, local party organs hardly exist beyond organizational charts. While party organizations are thus lacking, their activities are taken over by the two organizational entities: personal support organizations (koenkai) and intraparty factions (habatsu).

Koenkai

Koenkai are constituency groups organized as personal support organizations to back individual legislators. Masao Soma[5] has stated that every LDP member of the Diet has an individual koenkai that provides political backing, quite apart from another type that serves as a channel of financial aid from the economic community. In general, national labor unions function as koenkai for Socialist members of the Diet, although it is not unusual for the Socialist members connected with the Japan Farmers' Union to have their own koenkai. Even when a party branch exists in the Japanese countryside, it is likely to be part and parcel of an individual Diet member's koenkai.

Koenkai operate very much like the home offices of European members of parliament or U.S. congressmen, but with one significant difference. In Japan, constituents are encouraged to make their demands known indirectly through local organizations of koenkai rather than directly to the office of the Diet members. At any rate, constituents make their interests known to their representatives, and representatives distribute largess to their constituents through koenkai. Thus, they are ready-made bases for campaign organizations and other electoral activities for the Dietmen. They also appeal to local politicians, who generally constitute a nucleus of the koenkai leadership and benefit from the koenkai organization as well. Koenkai, based on particularized patterns of personal leadership, may indeed be a substitute model for party organization (see Chapter 5).

Since organizational units of the LDP seldom extend below its headquarters in the 47 prefectures and since the Socialist Party and the other lesser parties are primarily urban, koenkai dominate in rural Japan as functional grass-roots political groups loyal to individual legislators rather than to parties. According to Tadashi Yoshimura,[6] the LDP was, in the early 1960s, able to claim only 5,000 members in Ibaragi, a prefecture of more than 2 million inhabitants, and of these members, only 10 percent (that is, about 500) paid party dues. Parallel situations exist elsewhere in Japan. Given such minimal membership, it is very difficult for the LDP to establish and maintain viable grass-roots organizations. The answer to the difficulty seems to be koenkai.

Habatsu

Another operational political unit in Japan that functions like major party organizations is the intraparty faction, or habatsu, a characteristic feature of all Japanese political parties except Komeito. The LDP has had eight to 13 factions. The Socialist Party consists of several factions representing varied shades of socialist orientation. In 1960, it was from the Socialist Party that the right-wing Nishio faction splintered off in order to form the

TABLE 2.9

Opponents in Competition Perceived by the Winning Candidates of the 1967 General Election for the House of Representatives

Competitors	Liberal Democratic Party	Japan Socialist Party	Democratic Socialist Party	Komeito	Japan Communist Party	Total Number
One's own party candidates						
Number	94	36	1	0	0	131
Percent	44.5	30.5	4.6	0	0	
Other party's (ies') candidates						
Number	23	33	16	17	4	93
Percent	10.9	27.9	64.0	80.9	100.0	
One's own and other party's (ies') candidates						
Number	24	17	1	0	0	42
Percent	11.3	14.4	4.0	0	0	

Category		(1)	(2)	(3)	(4)	(5)	Total
Other party's (ies') and one's own candidates	Number	6	9	0	1	1	16
	Percent	2.8	7.6	0	4.7	0	
Not able to make distinctions	Number	10	5	2	1	1	18
	Percent	4.7	4.2	8.0	4.7	0	
Unknown	Number	54	18	5	1	0	79
	Percent	25.5	15.2	20.0	9.5	0	
Total	Number	211	118	25	21	4	379
	Percent	100.0	100.0	100.0	100.0	100.0	

Source: Hajime Shinohara and Yoshinori Ide, "Images of Elections Held by the Successful Candidates: The Case of Japan in 1967" (Paper presented to the 7th World Congress, Brussels, Belgium, of the International Political Science Association, September 1967).

Democratic Socialist Party. An aspect of this factionalized structure of Japanese politics may be observed in Table 2.9, which
shows the degree of intraparty struggle that prevails.

Shortly after the 1967 general election for the House of Representatives, when candidates were asked whom they considered to
have been their chief rivals in the election, 44.5 percent of the LDP
winners and about one-third of the Socialist victors cited members
of their own parties, whereas only 10.9 percent of the LDP winners
and 27.9 percent of the Socialists cited the candidates of other parties.[7] Though none of the Communists cited members of their own
party as rivals (in any case, they run only one candidate per district), factionalism in the Communist Party is also well documented.
We look at factionalism within the LDP in Chapter 4. Scalapino and
Masumi perceptively describe the Japanese party system, especially the two major parties, as "a system of loosely structured federa-
tions, each of which is composed of several semi-autonomous
'parties'."[8]

Scholars have discussed various causes of factionalism in
Japanese politics: historical tradition, postwar financial fragmentation, internal party composition, electoral arrangements, and
election of the party head, particularly the president of the LDP.
We shall discuss these causes below; here, two points are relevant.
First, although in the Socialist Party, factionalism has ideological
overtones, the factional relationship in Japan is primarily personal
and direct, centered upon allegiance owed directly to an individual
leader and not to the faction as such nor to the party as a whole.
Second, the faction functions very much like an independent party.
For example, LDP candidates are recruited through intraparty factions, and no faction puts up more than one candidate per district;
thus, several LDP candidates representing different factions may
be running for election in the same district. Under these circumstances, electoral campaigns tend to be conducted along factional
lines. Meanwhile, factional leaders are responsible not only for
recruiting candidates for party nominations but, also, for providing
campaign funds. Moreover, it is factional affiliation that deter-
mines advancement in both government and party, for it is thought
that a judicious balance of factions must be maintained among all
cabinet posts, vice-ministers (political), and committee chairmen
in the Diet, as well as among all officials of the party. It is factional leaders who determine the basic internal and external policies
of all parties except Komeito. Even in the Socialist Party, factional
alignment is important in the selection of candidates and party officials. Finally, it is factional coalitions of the LDP that determine
who becomes prime minister, because the president of the majority
party in the Diet automatically becomes premier (see Chapter 3 for
detailed analysis).

Parties and Supporting Interest Groups

Though its major support comes from rural areas, the LDP primarily represents the interests of Japanese business, particularly big business. A study made in the late 1950s indicated that over one-half of all conservative members of the Diet had close connections with business,[9] and the situation has not changed much in the last two decades. It is well known that big business provides the Liberal Democrats with a great deal, if not almost all, of their political and campaign funds, a considerable portion of which is channeled through Kokuminseijikyokai ("The Citizens' Political Association"), but the rest of which is given directly to various factional leaders or to individual Diet members. While each faction has its own financial sponsors, the Japanese financial community especially favors "bureaucratic factions" (that is, factions led by former higher civil servants), as the large contributions they have made to the old Ikeda, Sato, and Fukuda factions attest. The LDP is not unmindful of farm interests, but its foremost commitment is clearly to the business community and financial circles.

Japanese business has not attempted, however, to pursue its interests so directly as to offer its own candidates—that is, men drawn from its own ranks—for election to the Diet. Rather, preferring to work indirectly, it has chiefly relied upon former higher bureaucrats of the national government, who become members of the Diet upon their retirement and demonstrate in their new offices a willingness to serve their erstwhile associates in the private sector. Indeed for some time, retiring members of the Japanese higher civil service have been the major source of supply for LDP membership in the Diet. The pattern is striking. In 1953, ex-bureaucrats held 25 percent of the House membership of the Liberal Party, a conservative predecessor of the LDP, and after the 1958 elections, they held 26 percent of the House membership of the LDP. The situation was similar after the 1963 general election for the House of Representatives. In more recent years, one out of every four Liberal Democrats in the House of Representatives (1967, 26 percent; 1969, 25 percent; 1972, 23 percent; and 1976, 28 percent) and more than one out of every three newly elected members in the House of Councillors have been former government officials (1968, 38 percent; 1971, 40 percent; 1974, 39 percent; and 1977, 32 percent).

Not only do these ex-bureaucrats comprise a large segment of the LDP membership of the Diet, but they also hold positions of leadership both in the government and in the party. Because of their close contacts with incumbent bureaucrats, expert knowledge of public policy, and first-rate financial connections (which are indispensable to leaders of factions), they rise rapidly in the government and party hierarchy. Significantly, in 30-odd years of postwar cabinet history, in only a few years have cabinets been headed by prime ministers who do not have bureaucratic backgrounds. From 1955 to 1977, well over one-third of Japanese cabinet ministers were former government officials. As shown in Table 2.10, these ex-bureaucrats-turned-politicians hold important ministerial posts. Even this table does not indicate the real significance of "ex-bureaucrats," because not only do a far greater number of them hold ministerships longer than "nonbureaucrats," but they are also more frequent repeaters. A similar trend can be seen with respect to party posts. (See Appendix A.)

It is evident, then, that members of the LDP and members of the Japanese higher civil service are intimately linked. Quite apart from their migration into the party upon retirement, higher bureaucrats necessarily have daily contacts with party leaders, for, as the ruling party, the LDP utilizes the bureaucrats to the fullest possible extent in the formulation of its public policies. Before they can be presented to the cabinet, all government bills must first receive the approval of the Policy Affairs Research Council (Seimuchosakai), the decision-making arm of the party, the meetings of which higher civil servants often attend and within which they are said to wield tremendous influence. Since the standing committees of the Diet parallel the ministerial divisions of the government, more often than not, they are chaired by precisely those men who once held office in the very ministries they are supposed to supervise. It is not surprising, then, that some observers argue that the LDP is more dependent upon the bureaucracy than the bureaucracy on it.

Of course, the bureaucracy and business have always been intimately related. In addition to their day-to-day contacts and their frequent meetings in the milieu of lavish entertainment so prevalent in Japan, many higher bureaucrats actually join their business associates upon retirement by taking positions in the private economy. Yujiro Shinoda observed that by 1967, approximately 150 former bureau directors and vice-ministers (administrative) from the Ministry of International Trade and Industry alone sat on the executive boards of private companies.[10] Likewise, just for a period from 1970 to 1980, 173 ex-bureaucrats from the Ministry of Finance became executives of private banks and trust and stock companies, as well as of government-related financial organizations and other related public corporations. In 1966 alone, retiring bureaucrats from the Ministry of International Trade and Industry joined, among other companies, Yawata Steel, Shell Oil, Mobil Oil, and Hitachi Shipbuilding; others from the Ministry of Transportation joined Iino Shipping Lines, Kawasaki Steamship, Morita Steamship, Meitetsu-Tokyo Sightseeing Bus, and Toyonaka Taxi; and still others from the

TABLE 2.10

Number of Ex-bureaucrats Holding Cabinet Posts
from 1955 to 1977

Cabinet Post	Number of Ministers	Ex-bureaucrats	Percent
Prime Minister	8	4	50
Minister of Justice	21	11	52
Minister of Foreign Affairs	13	8	62
Minister of Finance	10	6	60
Minister of Education	17	8	47
Minister of Health and Welfare	22	11	50
Minister of Agriculture and Forestry	17	6	35
Minister of International Trade and Industry	18	9	50
Minister of Transportation	25	10	40
Minister of Post and Telecommunications	24	9	38
Minister of Labor	19	3	16
Minister of Construction	21	3	14
Minister of Autonomy	24	9	38
Director of Economic Planning Agency	18	9	50
Director of Defense Agency	22	10	46
Others	81	26	32
Total	360	142	39

Sources: Shugiin jimukyoru (House of Representatives Secretariat), Shugiin yōran [House of Representatives Digest] (Tokyo: Government Printing Office); Sangiin jimukyoku (House of Councillors Secretariat), Sangiin yōran [House of Councillors Digest (Directory)] (Tokyo: Government Printing Office), and Jinji Koshin roku [Who's Who] (1955-77).

Ministry of Construction joined Sato Industry, Taisei Construction, Kajima Construction, and Fujitagumi.[11] Others retiring from the Ministry of Health and Welfare have entered pharmaceutical firms. Former governmental officials also held the presidencies of many famous Japanese companies.*[12] In short, the LDP, the higher bureaucracy of the government, and Japanese business are intimately and significantly interrelated. Indeed, it is this tightly bound triple alliance that has been chiefly instrumental in the maintenance of conservative dominance in postwar Japan.[13]

By contrast, the Socialist Party speaks for labor, particularly organized labor. To be more precise, it primarily represents the interests of a single interest group, called the General Council of Trade Unions of Japan, known in Japanese as Sohyo. Although there are others, Sohyo is by far the largest federation of labor unions in the country. With a claimed membership of 4,525,237 in 1978, Sohyo includes not only workers from the private sectors of the economy but, also, a large majority of governmental workers. Some of its affiliates are the All-Japan Prefectural and Municipal Workers' Union, the Japan Teachers' Union, the Railway Workers, the National Postal Workers' Union and National Telecommunications Workers, the Japan Coal Miners, and the Federation of Private Railway Workers.

While all labor parties are allied with unions in one way or another, the alliance between the Socialist Party and Sohyo is so unusually close that the party has been called the "Political Department of Sohyo" or "Sohyo Party." Moreover, it is true that certain Sohyo organizational units often seem to replace the organizationally weak units of the party. During election campaigns, for example, Sohyo provides the party not only with candidates from among its own officers and campaign workers from among its own ranks but, also, political contributions from its own treasury, besides mobilizing its members to vote Socialist.

Accordingly, more than one-half of the Socialist members of the House of Representatives in recent years have been labor union

---

*For example, in one representative year, 1967, Sanyo Pulp, Tokyo-keiki, Nihongoseigomu, Nihon Denshikeisanki, Nissan Chemistry, Yawata Steel, Nihon Soda, Hokkaido Electric, Central Glass, Tohoku Railway, Showa Kaiun, International Telephone and Telegraph, Zenkoku Express, Nippon Express, Nankai Railway, Japan Travel Bureau, Japan Airlines, Nihon Shokudo, Yokohama Bank, Bank of Tokyo, and Saitama Bank had a former governmental official as president of their company.

officials (for example, as of February 1977, 65 percent), mostly of ex-governmental or public workers. In the House of Councillors, a significant majority of its Socialist members claim to have come up through the ranks of labor unions as well. For instance, after the July 1977 House of Councillors election, 59 percent of the newly elected members of the party were former labor union executives. Many Socialists in both houses of the Diet are actually former Sohyo executives. Even non-Sohyo Socialist members owe a great deal to the organization for their nomination and election, for Sohyo members make up approximately 70 percent of the membership of the Socialist Party, enough to control its convention. Further, Sohyo raises almost all of the party's campaign expenses.[14]

It is therefore not surprising that Socialist members of the Diet have close ties with Sohyo unions. To cite only a few examples, a considerable number of the Socialist members of its Education Committee are associated with the Japan Teachers' Union, some Socialist members of its Transportation Committee with various unions connected with transportation, and Socialist members of the Postal and Communications Committee to the National Postal Workers' Union and National Telecommunications Workers. It is reported that the Socialist Party and Sohyo maintain an office for their Joint Diet-Struggle Committee even inside the Diet building, that the director of Sohyo's Political Department stays there during legislative sessions in order to further Sohyo's interests, and that the party must get the approval of the committee before negotiating with the ruling LDP on any matter related to the unions or to Sohyo at large. It is rare to find a party anywhere that is as tightly restricted by its supporters as the Japan Socialist Party.[15]

Recently, two tendencies in the Sohyo-Socialist Party relationship have developed. One is the weakening of Sohyo leadership control of its rank and file members, as a move against exclusive support of the Socialist Party is underway among Sohyo affiliates, and to make the situation more complicated, there is much talk of labor realignment in the 1970s along more moderate lines. The other trend has to do with the nature and age of Socialist candidates for election and members of the Diet. Because Sohyo often uses Diet seats as sinecures for its officials, who are pushed out by federation policy to make way for new federation leadership, many Socialist candidates not only come from the executive posts of labor unions, but are older.[16]

Like the Socialist Party, the Democratic Socialist Party represents the interests of labor, but not exclusively. In fact, the party claims that because it is supported by three social pillars—workers, farmers, and small- and medium-sized entrepreneurs (shop owners)— it is a people's party (Kokuminseito), not a protector of the working

class only. While it is true that the party does not maintain monop-
olistic relations with its union associates, but represents other interests as well, the nucleus of its support comes from the Japanese
Confederation of Labor, or <u>Domei</u>, which reported a membership
of 2,181,810 workers as of June 1978.

Domei is politically moderate in comparison to Sohyo. Some
of its affiliates are the Japan Federation of Textile Workers' Unions,
the All Japan Seamen's Union, the National Federation of Metal Industry Trade Unions, the Japanese Federation of Chemical and General Workers' Union, and the Federation of Electric Workers'
Unions of Japan. Having won most of its affiliates from private industry, Domei is the second largest federation of unions in Japan.[17]

Domei was founded in the fall of 1964 as a consolidation of
various labor groups that were consistent backers of right-wing
socialism. Although the exact measure of its support of the Democratic Socialist Party is difficult to assess, certainly the party
could not have survived without it. Domei people are reported to
participate actively in the party's decision-making processes, and
many of its prefectural offices are identical with those of the party.
Domei often provides the party's candidates for elections; it is also
the principal source of the party's campaign workers and monetary
funds. Without its support, a Democratic Socialist candidate would
have a hard time winning a seat in the Diet.

However, the Democratic Socialist Party has seldom been
charged, as has the Socialist Party, with "selling out" to its union
supporters. The reason may be that Domei, committed as it is to
"democratic unionism," refuses to subjugate its economic purposes
to political ones or to let its economic struggles become politicized.
In fact, leaving political matters to the Democratic Socialists, while
addressing itself almost exclusively to economic matters, Domei
has openly criticized its counterpart Sohyo for operating like a
political party.

Komeito is the political arm of the religious organization
Sokagakkai, which claimed a membership of 7.75 million Japanese
households in 1975, the latest figure available. Although the two
entities are ostensibly separate, officially severing their ties in
1970, almost all of the workers, leaders, and candidates of Komeito
are members of Sokagakkai. Not only is it difficult to distinguish
members of the one organization from members of the other, because identical persons play dual roles in both organizations, but
the leadership of the two organizations is closely interlocked (see
Appendix A, Tables A.2 and A.3, which indicate Komeito membership both in the Diet and in Sokagakkai as of 1969, prior to the
separation). In 1969, Komeito held 47 seats in the House of Representatives, where it ranked third, and in 1972, 29 seats in the House

of Representatives, where it ranked fourth. In 1976, the party regained the third-party position in the House of Representatives with 55 members; in 1979, it increased the number of seats it held by two. In 1980, its percentage of seats declined slightly. It has approximately 3,300 legislators (1977) throughout the country, mostly local assemblymen, where the party's real strength lies.

The phenomenal growth and electoral success of Komeito in its very short history can be attributed to its very strong grassroots base in Sokagakkai, whose organization is highly effective because of both its discipline and militancy. Essentially embracing the principle of the union of church (Buddhism) and state, the members of Sokagakkai thus endeavor to enhance the well-being not only of themselves as individuals but, also, of society as a whole. As Kasahara has put it, "an order issued by Sokagakkai leaders seems identical with the commands of the Savior and can move (the membership) accordingly."[18] Given this formidable unity, Komeito leaders can often predict exactly the votes their candidates will receive; their electoral arrangements, which provide for prearranged numbers of votes per bloc, work so successfully that in this respect at least, the party is the envy of all its rivals. Furthermore, as we have noted previously, the Japanese electoral system of multi-member districts favors minor parties like Komeito, because they can concentrate on one candidate per district, while major parties have difficulty optimally apportioning the votes of their supporters among several candidates.

Some distinctive aspects of Komeito supporters are indicated in Table 2.11. Apparently the party attracts more women than men, more younger persons than older persons, more unorganized manual laborers and workers in small- and medium-sized businesses than other kinds of workers, and more persons with less than secondary education than with higher education.[19] These findings, as well as others, especially electoral results in Tokyo areas, tend to support the generalization that the foundation of the party extends from the urban lower middle class to the middle class. An empirical study made by Nara indicates that Komeito rather than the Communist Party has performed best in districts characterized by low income and low levels of education.[20]

By appealing to the interests of the lower middle and other middle classes that rival parties have failed to protect, Komeito seems to have adequate room for advancement in the 1970s and 1980s. Because of the religious motivations and central direction that it shares with Sokagakkai, the party will probably continue to mobilize the votes of its followers as effectively in the future as in the past. However, Komeito, like the Communist Party, appears to evoke strong negative sentiment among many voters, especially

TABLE 2.11

Social Background of the Komeito Supporters
(percent)

Background	National Average	Osaka Prefecture[a]	Kochi Prefecture[b]	Total Eligible Votes—Average
Sex				
Male	41	47	30	47
Female	59	53	70	53
Age				
20–29	23	28	12	24
30–39	25	29	24	26
40–49	23	21	34	19
50–59	14	14	18	16
60+	15	8	12	15
Occupation				
White-collar	17	8	9	24
Blue-collar	15	20	0	16
Other laborers, mainly day workers	30	37	36	14
Small proprietors	19	30	15	19
Primary industrial workers	11	2	40	24
Others (including housewives)	6	2	0	3
Years of Education				
0–6	27			20
7–9	45			43
10–12	23			29
13	5			8

[a]Osaka Prefecture is taken as an example of an urban area.
[b]Kochi Prefecture is taken as an example of a rural area.
Source: Editorial staff, "Komeito no Taishitsu to Kino," Asahi janaru [Asahi journal], March 5, 1967, p. 14.

in urban areas, where its strength rests, which may place upper limits on its voter appeal.[21]

SUMMARY

All Japanese political parties are closely tied up with various economic or religious interests, more often than not with single-interest groups—the LDP with business and higher bureaucracy, the Japan Socialist Party with Sohyo, the Democratic Socialist Party with Domei, Komeito with Sokagakkai, and the Communist Party, although not discussed here, with its well-known ideological cause.[22] Often substituting functionally for the parties themselves, their supporting organizations are instrumental in the selection of party officials, the recruitment of party workers and candidates, and the funding of campaign activities. "Because Japanese political parties have not performed their intrinsic political functions," writes Masao Maruyama, "the vacuum has been filled by labor unions and other organizations, whose original objectives were the carrying out of economic struggles."[23] Indeed, when such interest groups do not assume party functions, habatsu (intraparty factions) or koenkai do so. Particularly in the case of the LDP, which has held power most of the time in postwar Japan, intraparty factions have perhaps functioned effectively as internal checks. Yet it should be remembered that both intraparty factions and koenkai are the political machines of individual politicians and essentially perpetuate the personalized nature of Japanese political life.

Several questions of importance related to the political party process emerge out of our discussion of postwar trends in voter participation and party support patterns, as well as organizational and socio-interest bases of Japanese political parties. To what extent are the patterns of voting participation and party support related to the style and content of political party institutionalization? What is the relationship between urbanization and voter participation? What are some of the consequences of various aspects of party institutionalization on the future electoral alignment? To be more specific, how are the patterns of party support for the LDP, Japan Socialist Party, Democratic Socialist Party, Japan Communist Party, and Komeito related to various indexes of social development, like urbanization, industrialization, and education?

Why are factions and koenkai important elements in the political process, if indeed they are? Factions and koenkai are endogenous models that are supportive of the hierarchical style of authority and decision making noted by observers to characterize Japanese society. We shall attempt to answer these questions below.

So far, then, we have descriptive evidence that individual political parties are mainly organized around specialized support bases or, in the case of the LDP, koenkai, a traditional-type support base. This description presents a picture of reasonable stability and perhaps offers support for adherents of the corporate vision of Japanese society and politics.

NOTES

1. Nonelectoral figures appearing in this chapter are taken from appropriate editions of Asahi nenkan, most notably of 1977; unless otherwise noted, biographical data are from various editions of Shugiin yōran and Sangiin yōran [House of Representatives and House of Councillors surveys] and Kokai-binran [Diet handbook]. For sources of electoral figures, see Appendix B.

2. For excellent accounts of prewar Japanese political party change, see Robert A. Scalapino, Democracy and the Party Movement in Prewar Japan: The Failure of the First Attempt (Berkeley and Los Angeles: University of California Press, 1953); Peter Duus, Party Rivalry and Political Change in Taisho Japan (Cambridge, Mass.: Harvard University Press, 1968); and Junnosuke Masumi, Nihon Seitoshi-ron [A history of Japanese political parties], vols. 1-5 (Tokyo: Tokyo University Press, 1965-79). Compare Tetsuo Najita, Hara Kei and the Politics of Compromise (Cambridge, Mass.: Harvard University Press, 1967).

3. Junichi Kyogoku and Nobutaka Ike, "Urban-rural Differences in Voting Behavior in Postwar Japan," The Proceedings of the Department of Social Sciences, College of General Education, no. 9 (Tokyo: University of Tokyo, 1959), mimeographed; Robert E. Ward, "Urban-Rural Differences and the Process of Political Modernization in Japan: A Case Study," Economic Development and Cultural Change 9 (October 1960), pt. II, pp. 135-65; Joji Watanuki, "Social Structure and Political Participation in Japan" (Tokyo: Institute of International Relations, Sophia University, 1972); compare also Bradley M. Richardson, "Urbanization and Political Participation: The Case of Japan," American Political Science Review 67 (June 1973): 433-52.

4. Robert E. Ward, Japan's Political System, 2d ed. (Englewood Cliffs, N.J.: Prentice-Hall, 1978), p. 73. Compare James White, Sokagakkai: The Politics of Mass Society (Stanford, Calif.: Stanford University Press, 1971).

5. Masao Soma, Nihon no senkyo [Japanese elections] (Tokyo: Usho Shuppansha, 1967); see also Nihon seiji-gakkai (Japanese Political Science Association), ed., Gendai nihon no seitō to kanryō (Tokyo: Iwanami Shoten, 1967), p. 142.

6. Tadashi Yoshimura, Nihon seiji no shindan [A diagnosis of Japanese politics] (Tokyo: Seishin Shobō, 1964), pp. 136-37; N. B. Thayer (translated by Katsumi Kobayashi), Jiminto (Tokyo: Sekkasha, 1968), pp. 71-74; N. B. Thayer, How the Conservatives Rule Japan (Princeton, N.J.: Princeton University Press, 1969).

7. Hajime Shinohara and Yoshinori Ide, "Images of Election Held by the Successful Candidates: The Case of Japan in 1967" (Paper presented to 7th World Congress, Brussels, of the International Political Science Association convention, September 1967). Our data on the prefectural assemblymen (in Kanagawa, Yamanashi, and Shimane prefectures) also corroborate this pattern.

8. Robert A. Scalapino and Junnosuke Masumi, Parties and Politics in Contemporary Japan (Berkeley and Los Angeles: University of California Press, 1962), p. 79.

9. Ibid., pp. 63-167.

10. Yujiro Shinoda, "Management Associations and Government Agencies in Japan" (Tokyo: Sophia University, Socio-Economic Institute, 1967), mimeographed, p. 102; Asahi Shimbun [Asahi Newspaper] Tokyo, February 10, 1980.

11. Hirotatsu Fujiwara, "A Report on the Higher Bureaucrats' AMAKUDARI," Shinpyo (September 1967), pp. 53-54.

12. Ibid.; Shinoda, "Management Associations and Government Agencies in Japan"; see also Akira Kubota, Higher Civil Servants in Postwar Japan (Princeton, N.J.: Princeton University Press, 1969), pp. 140-95.

13. For a fuller discussion of this topic, see Kan Ori, "The Japanese Higher Bureaucracy" (Paper presented to the International Management Development Seminar, Tokyo, September 1969), and Nihon seiji-gakkai (Japanese Political Science Association), ed., Gendai nihon no seitō to kanryō.

14. Various editions of Kokkai-binran; Tatsuo Nakano and Shigetaro Iizuka, Shakaitō-Minshatō [The Japan Socialist Party and the Democratic Socialist Party] (Tokyo: Sekkasha, 1968).

15. Nakano and Iizuka, Shakaitō-Minshatō, p. 94. A more reserved view is expressed by Allan B. Cole, George O. Totten, and Cecil R. Uyehara, Socialist Parties in Postwar Japan (New Haven, Conn.: Yale University Press, 1966), p. 354: "These committees have attempted to coordinate economic struggles with political strategy, especially with the advocacy of, and opposition to, controversial legislation; but they can make no binding decisions."

16. Cole, Totten, and Uyehara, Socialist Parties in Postwar Japan, p. 97; Sigeki Nishihira, "Senkyo kara mita kakuto no genjyo to shorai [The present situation and the future of each party viewed from the general elections], Tenbo (April 1967): 57.

17. These figures and other data on labor statistics are from Rodosho (Ministry of Labor), Rodo tokei nenkan [Labor statistical

yearbook] (Tokyo: Rodosho, 1977), and Asahi nenkan [Asahi year-book] (Tokyo: Asahi Shimbunsha, 1979).

18. Kazuo Kasahara, "Soka Gakkai and Komeito," Japan Quarterly 14 (October 1967): 311.

19. Editorial Staff, "Komeito no taishitsu to kino," Asahi janaru [Asahi Journal] 19 (March 5, 1967): 13-14.

20. See Moriyoshi Nara, Analysis of Voting Behavior in Tokyo Areas, Minshushugi Kenkyu-kai (1966), pp. 1-118; on Komeito/Sokagakkai, consult, for example, James W. White, Sokagakkai: The Politics of Mass Society (Stanford, Calif.: Stanford University Press, 1971).

21. In a recent study, respondents were asked: "Do you have in mind a party which you do not wish to support at any cost? If so, which party is it?" Usually, close to 30 percent of the respondents named the Japan Communist Party as a veto party, while Komeito was so considered by 10 to 20 percent of them in the urban areas. (See, for example, the 1972 survey findings of the Institute of International Relations, Sophia University, Tokyo; Keizo Okabe and Joji Watanuki, Kokusai ishiki chōsa [International political consciousness survey] (Tokyo: 1968, mimeographed); and various surveys of Komei senkyo renmei (Clean Election Federation).

22. For works on the Japan Communist Party, see Robert A. Scalapino, The Japanese Communist Movement, 1920-1966 (Berkeley and Los Angeles: University of California Press, 1976); George M. Beckmann and Genji Okubo, The Japanese Communist Party (Stanford, Calif.: Stanford University Press, 1969); and Paul F. Langer, Communism in Japan (Stanford, Calif.: Hoover Institution Press, 1972).

23. Quoted in Hajime Shinohara and Yonosuke Nagai, eds., Gendai seijigaku nyumon [An introduction to contemporary political science] (Tokyo: Yuhikaku, 1965), p. 144.

3
PARTY CHANGE IN JAPANESE ELECTORAL POLITICS

THE PROBLEM

Let us see if we can reorient discussion of the process of
Japanese political party change at the prefectural level. Employing
regression analysis on over time aggregate data, we shall examine
the 11 elections from 1952 to 1979. The chapter is an exploration
of the contribution of statistical analysis to our examination of political party change.

Despite the growing amount and quality of work on Japanese
political parties, voting participation, and their relationship to
socioeconomic change, a good deal of confusion about the subject
remains.[1] Some authors see the political party system in transition;[2] others view it as stable.[3] The LDP is either declining or
maintaining surprising strength in the face of rapid socioeconomic
change.[4] For comparative political party theorists, Japan exhibits
a political party system with a high level of institutionalization.[5]
Japanese specialists view the same party system as in transition,
development, and so forth. From work in cross-national comparative analysis, we learn there is a positive relationship between
measures of socioeconomic development and political development
in general and voting participation[6] and of political party development in particular.[7] We learn from application of the same methodology to the Japanese case that the same finding is reversed. The
higher the level of urbanization, the lower the level of voting. The
higher the level of socioeconomic development, the lower the level
of party competition.[8]

What accounts for these contradictions and disparities? Is
Japan that different from other postindustrial states? Or is it in
the comparisons that one must look to for the answer? Perhaps

studies on Japan are invalid, or perhaps it is the cross-national-based work—or both. While this is not the place to discuss the central theory and method difficulties inherent in cross-national theory construction efforts, the way the comparativists and Japan specialists have proceeded has set the agenda of problems to study incorrectly; we turn to summarize this work.

BACKGROUND

Urbanization and Voting Participation

Stimulated by work done by U.S. specialists,[9] comparativists and their counterparts working on Japan have examined the relationships between place of residence and political participation. Studies, ably synthesized by Richardson,[10] show clearly that political participation has been higher in rural than in urban districts at all levels. Richardson sees this finding as running counter to modernization theory, which, as he puts it, would "anticipate higher levels of political involvement and participation in urban areas."[11] Still, as Richardson himself notes, the role of tradition is frequently cited as the primary explanation of this relationship. The Japanese version of the social net theory suggests that where the traditional bonds of leader-follower relationships (Oyabun-kobun) and group cohesion ties remain strong, individual compliance with the leader's desires is high. This situation is most likely to be found in the buraku ("hamlet") in the rural areas.

We would make two points with respect to this finding. The first, and more limited, is that employment of nonlinear techniques of analysis yields a significant alteration of the finding when measured by voting.[12] Voting rose (the 1967 election) from the prefectures with the lowest levels of urbanization to moderate levels of urbanization before falling off rapidly. The second concerns the explanation of this finding. Instead of relying on tradition, it appears to us that a more interesting line to investigate is the relationship between political participation and political party institutionalization. Where party institutionalization is high, voting participation may be high; where voting participation is low, political party institutionalization may be low.[13] We shall discuss and define the party institutionalization concept below, but first let us turn briefly to a discussion of the work of the dominant Japanese modernization and party change school to date.

Modernization and Japanese Political
Party Institutionalization

Most Japan specialists see the Japan political party system as underdeveloped or in transition.

We do not think it is helpful to characterize the Japanese political party system as traditional[14] or developing[15] unless the endpoints of such characterization are provided. The Japanese party system may be in transition, but from what to what? If, for example, by party system underdevelopment, the author means party system instability, should not investigation be made in order to discover the empirical pattern of party system change? Because observers have seen the LDP as representing the forces of conservative tradition and because its vote shares have declined, the continued decline of the LDP and the rise of the change-("modern") oriented parties of the left has been predicted. But we need to look at the empirical pattern here as well. As we attempt to show below, the LDP is enjoying success in substituting koenkai for party organization. There are two points to be made here also. Can we bring empirical evidence to bear on this question? Is the observation correct? If so, where do the koenkai organizations tend to emerge?

THE PARTY SYSTEM: CONCEPT FORMATION
AND PROCESS ANALYSIS

We shall conceive of Japanese political party institutionalization as based on assumptions about party system institutionalization, which differ from conventional assumptions about political party development, and present empirical evidence on hypotheses developed around this concept. First, we need to recognize that the Japanese political party system must be viewed as more than its constituent parts:

> . . . the network of competitive relationships between
> political parties. The party system is not literally a
> collection of parties—men, institutions, and activities.
> It is instead the competition between these parties
> within a single political regime . . . the party system
> is the matrix of competitive relationships between these
> parties. The party system is the whole assortment of
> interparty rivalries in a single country at any single
> time.[16]

While there are several ways of attempting to capture the party institutionalization concept, we shall, with Przezworski and Sprague,[17] refer simply to the relative <u>stability</u> of particular patterns of behavior over time as more accurately capturing the core of the institutionalization concept, which rests on the notion of the degree of stable, enduring patterns of behavior. Therefore, we shall treat Japanese party system institutionalization as the degree of stability of competitive patterns. This requires over time analysis and necessitates making a number of simplifying assumptions.

First, we shall operate with subnational prefectural units of analysis. Aggregating electoral behavior at the national level masks cross-cutting variation at the subnational level. In a society where rapid socioeconomic change is occurring, there may be considerable variation across the 47 prefectures in terms of both the differential levels of socioeconomic development and the rate of the change itself. Second, we shall rest our argument on aggregate data that pose both possibilities and problems. In addition to the standard cross-level inference and ecological fallacy problems, we may not use our ecological data base to examine the interesting changing patterns of party identification support.

We have argued elsewhere[18] that ecological information is invaluable for the development and testing of system-level hypotheses, and that is the case especially when we introduce the third assumption we shall use to guide our analysis.

To begin with, we assume that there is a regular identifiable process of political party change. Thus, we assume that Japanese political parties are at a particular point in this change process. The problem is that we lack theory in the political party field sufficient to make much sense out of the cross-sectional studies that correlate socioeconomic development and voting participation or party institutionalization.[19] The devastating assumption that necessarily accompanies these studies is that the relationships in and among the variables examined are <u>stable</u> over time—and we know instinctively that <u>very</u> few social systems remain in such equilibrium. Apropos our earlier discussion of the findings on Japanese political parties, we do not really know if the relationships between urbanization or socioeconomic level of development and voting participation would hold up if we could introduce the party institutionalization variable. What about the differential effects of both different <u>levels</u> and of changing <u>rates</u> of socioeconomic factors on the party system? What about the competitive interaction between the parties themselves over time?

THE ANALYSIS

We shall examine all national elections to the House of Representatives from 1952, the point of resumption of national indepen-
dence, to 1979; the 46 prefectures will be the units of analysis.
(Okinawa was returned to Japan in time for the 1972 election, but
we do not include it here because there are no previous elections
from which over time comparisons can be made.) To undertake our
time series analysis, we shall employ a measure that allows us to
evaluate the models discussed above. The measure is,

$$H(P) = \sum_{i=1}^{N} p(i) \log_2 (1/p(i)) \text{ with } \sum_{i=1}^{N} p(i) = 1$$

where H equals the total degree of political party competition. P(i)
is the fraction of the total vote falling to the ith party in a N party
system. The higher the level of political party competition, meaning the more equal the shares of the vote p(i), the higher the level
of entropy. Thus, for us, the degree of party system institutionalization can be defined as the degree of change in entropy levels
over time. In other words, the less the change in entropy, the
greater the degree of party system stability and, for us, party system institutionalization. We shall also examine the major hypotheses
about the relationship between individual political parties and socioeconomic development measures. By calculating Hi (a decimal
fraction [i] of the vote) for specific parties, one may derive the
proportion of H(i) contributed to by the individual parties. Thus,
the measure controls for the number of parties that change across
elections. In order to assess the effects of mobilization, we will
use urbanization (population density per kilometer) as an independent variable.[20] Finally, koenkai (personal support organizations)
membership will be considered as a possible explanatory variable
of LDP support. Recent students of socioeconomic development,
political participation, and political party institutionalization now
divide their formulations into those based on levels of socioeconomic
development and rates of socioeconomic change. We shall make the
same division in order to examine the relative importance of levels
of socioeconomic development compared to rates of change in those
levels in postwar Japan. Table 3.1 presents entropy for the 11
elections analyzed. Before 1952, the number of political parties
and their respective vote shares fluctuated widely, as the Japanese
recovered from the effects of a political system breakdown at the

end of World War II and during the Occupation (which ended in 1952). These atypical years are excluded. Table 3.2 presents us with a series of entropy findings that allow us to evaluate the hypotheses about political party institutionalization. First, let us examine the absolute entropy levels over the 20-year span. The considerable decline in entropy from 1953 to 1958 is consistent with interpretations of the period. After the merger of the political parties of the left into the Japan Socialist Party and the formation of the LDP by the conservatives, there was a rapid decline in entropy, as illustrated in the 1958 election. From this low of 1.30 in 1958, entropy began to move upward again during the decade of the 1960s, reflecting the split off of part of the Socialist group into the Democratic Socialist Party (1960), the birth (1964) and growth of Komeito, which contested the House of Representatives elections for the first time in 1967, and the steady growth of the Japan Communist Party. But the major finding concerns the relative degree of party system institutionalization over the 11 elections. The entropy mean change rate of .19 over the 11 elections indicates a high degree of early system stability. This is particularly true if one controls for the one large rate entropy rate change of -.76 from 1955 to 1958. Individual party fluctuations may be lost, but the theoretical notion that the overall party system is in rapid change or transition seems questionable.

TABLE 3.1

Entropy Levels: Japan, 1952-79

Election Year	Mean Political Party System Entropy	Rate Entropy Change (from previous election)
1952	1.98	
1953	2.16	+.18
1955	2.06	-.10
1958	1.30	-.76
1960	1.46	+.16
1963	1.51	+.05
1967	1.61	+.10
1969	1.76	+.15
1972	1.77	+.01
1976	1.82	+.05
1979	1.85	+.03
	Mean rate of entropy change .19	

Source: Compiled by the authors.

TABLE 3.2

Political Party System Entropy, Voting Participation,
and Urbanization: Japan, 1952-79

Election Year	Beta Weights— Voting Participation*	Beta Weights— Urbanization*
1952	3.29	-1.96
1953	4.83	-4.12
1955	7.50	3.13
1958	2.62	-6.41
1960	1.60	-1.35
1963	6.70	-3.37
1967	5.74	-6.48
1969	9.38	-3.30
1972	9.70	-5.05
1976	9.73	-4.85
1979	8.94	-4.26

*Significant at the .95 confidence interval.
Source: Compiled by the authors.

A key question concerns the range of variation across the prefectures. Figure 3.1 presents the standard deviation of entropy for
the political party system over the 11 elections. Large standard
deviation scores would reflect higher degrees of heterogeneity
across the 46 prefectures. Lower standard deviation levels would
reflect homogeneity across the prefectures. Figure 3.1 suggests
that the trend has been toward homogenization of the prefectural
system.

We have noted that voting participation falls with urbanization.
Table 3.2 gives us a further opportunity to assess this and the voting-
participation-related hypothesis. By computing a multiple regression equation, we may compare urbanization and voting participation
over time. Beta coefficients may be interpreted as the proportion
of regression slope accounted for by the single independent variable.
Furthermore, we may use the beta coefficients in two distinct ways
in order to look at the difference between the effects of levels of
urbanization and voting participation and the process of rate changes
in these variables on party system institutionalization, as measured
by the change in entropy.

FIGURE 3.1

Standard Deviation of Political Party System Entropy

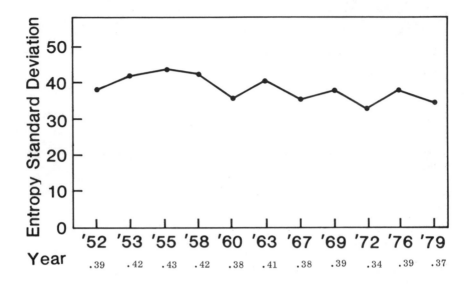

Source: Compiled by the authors.

We move, in Table 3.2, to examine the relationship between our measure of political party system entropy and our two independent variables—voting participation and urbanization. First, note the positive relationship between entropy and voting participation. Without exception, during the 27 years and 11 elections, we see that voting and entropy are related in a positive manner, and with the exception of the 1955 election, urbanization and entropy are related in a negative fashion.

We know from Tables 2.1 and 2.2 in Chapter 2 and Table 3.2 in this chapter that voting participation and urbanization are negatively related. However, continuing our examination of the differences between the political parties, for example, levels of party institutionalization as measured by entropy and individual political party proportions of entropy, we present the findings on the relationship between H(i) and urbanization, our mobilization variable (Table 3.3). The expected finding that the LDP is inversely related to urbanization while the other parties are related in a linear fashion is corroborated. It is interesting to reconfirm an earlier

TABLE 3.3

Political Party Entropy and Urbanization: Japan, 1955–79

Election Year	Liberal Democratic Party Beta Weights*	Japan Socialist Party Beta Weights	Japan Communist Party Beta Weights	Komei Party Beta Weights
1955	-4.71	7.93	3.33	—
1958	-6.19	-6.09	3.27	—
1960	-3.66	-6.40	2.29	—
1963	-5.43	7.25	4.50	—
1967	-2.33	-9.22	3.68	6.56
1969	-2.97	-1.20	6.56	5.47
1972	-9.65	5.86	2.33	2.41
1976	-4.23	-1.73	3.10	2.71
1979	-5.47	-2.54	5.23	3.62

*Significant at the .95 confidence interval.
Source: Compiled by the authors.

finding, namely, that the Japan Socialist Party draws its strength from the same rural areas that the LDP does, though it gained slightly more urban strength in the 1972 elections. This confirms the notion of many observers of Japanese politics that the Japan Socialist Party has been the traditional protest party, while the Japan Communist and Komei parties have emerged to capture the urban change-oriented sector.

What factors combine to explain the ability of the LDP to maintain itself and, thus, to some extent the party system as a whole to remain at a relatively consistent competitive level? There are several plausible explanations offered elsewhere.

The development and growth of koenkai has been offered as a partial explanation of the continued success of the LDP. In describing and defining koenkai in Chapter 2, we outlined an important endogenous institution that potentially may be used in concert with other "modern" organizational mobilization techniques. The voting support of the LDP remains relatively high. To what extent has it been able to employ koenkai as a substitute for local party organization? We present Table 3.4 to address this puzzle, and the answers are striking. Koenkai in this table is the percent reported to be in koenkai organizations across the 46 prefectures in 1972.[21] We place the voting participation and urbanization beta slopes next to koenkai for comparative purposes. The large positive beta weight for the LDP is in clear contrast to the negative scores of the other parties. When one further relates koenkai (Pearson Rs) to voting participation and urbanization, we see that koenkai and voter turnout are highly related. It is indeed the employment of this electoral support mechanism that aids the LDP.

CONCLUSION

This analysis is not a theory of Japanese political party system institutionalization. For that, we need a good deal more work to relate socioeconomic development, political participation, and party institutionalization. It may well be, for example, that we must examine the prewar period for evidence of the impact of rapid mobilization.

However, a study that evaluates evidence over a 20-year period is sufficient enough to at least cast doubts with respect to the major claims of both the comparative theorists and Japan specialist schools for the postwar period and suggests additional steps of inquiry.

TABLE 3.4

Relationship between Koenkai and Political Party
Entropy in 1972

Political Party	Koenkai Beta Weights*	Voting Participation Beta Weights	Urbanization Beta Weights
Liberal Democratic Party	8.60	-1.05	-9.66
Japan Socialist Party	-1.11	-7.48	5.87
Japan Communist Party	-1.41	-8.35	2.34
Komei Party	-1.21	-7.39	4.32

Pearson coefficient—Koenkai and voting participation, .83;
Koenkai and urbanization, .32

*Significant at the .95 confidence interval.
Source: Compiled by the authors.

Models of the Japanese electoral process based on modernization assumptions clearly have limited utility in the Japanese case.
Perhaps this was always the case, although we believe not, for in
the face of extremely rapid socioeconomic change, the party system achieved and then has maintained stability at a reasonably high
level. In a parallel manner, the pattern of support for the LDP
does not support the assumption that the Japanese party system is
particularly unique. The individual political party change process
gives evidence of a party system in movement, with the left parties
capturing major portions of the change-oriented sectors of Japan.
The pace of change in the LDP's proportion of the vote system is
much less than the opposition parties. Although we do not have
available data that would allow us to extend our analysis of the
koenkai, LDP strength, and urbanization to the 1976, 1979, and 1980
lower house elections, the election results do not contradict the
analysis and generalizations made here.

So we end with another set of questions. Will the LDP success
in developing koenkai continue in the face of still ongoing urbanization? Although we feel confident about our finding of the stability of

the Japanese political party system, we cannot claim that the actual level of entropy itself is small. How does the Japanese party system entropy compare with that of other political party systems over time?

By employment of such measurement procedures as entropy over time, within and between nation comparisons can aid in reformulating the way we think about the process of political party institutionalization itself, and this is the fundamental point.

How one interprets these findings depends on the framework used. Keying on the process assumption, we have chosen to look at the developmental relationships between the major political institutional dimensions, such as parties, as they relate to measures of political participation and socioeconomic change. Surely, the party system will undergo substantial future change in the next decade as the parties of the left finally engage in coalition behavior. But that change will come out of a legacy of substantial stability, which, itself, will hopefully serve as an effective midwife to the set of changes.

NOTES

1. We would like to thank Mitchell Joelson for valuable help in the preparation of the data for analysis.

2. Scott Flanagan, "The Japanese Party System in Transition," Comparative Politics 3 (January 1971): 230 ff.

3. Nathaniel B. Thayer, How the Conservatives Rule Japan (Princeton, N.J.: Princeton University Press, 1969).

4. Robert Scalapino and Junnosuke Masumi, Parties and Politics in Contemporary Japan (Berkeley and Los Angeles: University of California Press, 1962), and Sung-il Choi, "Systems Outputs, Social Environment, and Political Cleavages in Japan: The Case of the 1969 General Election," American Journal of Political Science 18 (February 1973): 99-122.

5. Kenneth Janda, A Conceptual Framework for the Comparative Analysis of Political Parties, Comparative Politics Series, vol. 1 (Beverly Hills, Calif.: Sage Publications, 1970).

6. S. M. Lipset, "Some Social Requisites of Democracy: Economic Development and Political Legitimacy," American Political Science Review 53, no. 1 (March 1959): 69-105; Samuel P. Huntington, Political Order in Changing Societies (New Haven, Conn.: Yale University Press, 1968).

7. Ibid.

8. Chong Lim Kim, "Socio-Economic Development and Political Democracy in Japanese Prefectures," American Political Science Review 65 (March 1971): 184-86.

9. Lester Milbrath, Political Participation (Chicago: Rand McNally, 1977).

10. Bradley M. Richardson, "Urbanization and Political Participation: The Case of Japan," American Political Science Review 67 (June 1973): 433-52.

11. Ibid., p. 434.

12. Roger W. Benjamin et al., Patterns of Political Development: Japan, India, Israel (New York: David McKay, 1972), p. 150.

13. Huntington, Political Order in Changing Societies.

14. Flanagan, "Japanese Party System in Transition."

15. See the articles in Robert E. Ward, ed., Political Development in Modern Japan (Princeton, N.J.: Princeton University Press, 1965).

16. Douglas W. Rae, Jr., The Political Consequences of Electoral Laws (New Haven, Conn.: Yale University Press, 1971), p. 47.

17. Adam Przeworski and John D. Sprague, "Concepts in Search of Explicit Formulation: A Study in Measurement," Midwest Journal of Political Science 15 (May 1971): 183-218; Huntington, Political Order in Changing Societies, chap. 1.

18. Benjamin et al., Patterns of Political Development, pp. 174-84.

19. Kim, "Socio-Economic Development and Political Democracy in Japanese Prefectures."

20. The sources for our data were as follows: (1) prefectural voting data, Shugiin jimukyoku (House of Representatives Secretariat), Shugiin giin sosenkyo ichiran [A report on the general elections for the House of Representatives] (Tokyo: House of Representatives Secretariat, 1948-73); (2) density per kilometer, Sōrifu tōkeikyoku (Bureau of Statistics, Office of the Prime Minister), Kokusai chōsa hōkoku [National Census report] (Tokyo: Tōkei Kyokai, 1950-72); and Sōrifu tōkeikyoku (Bureau of Statistics, Office of the Prime Minister), Nihon tōkei nenken [Japan statistical yearbook] (Tokyo: Nihon Tōkei Kyokai, 1950-72). The rationale for utilizing only urbanization as our mobilization (socioeconomic) variable concerns the extremely high degree of intercorrelation between measures of urbanization and other measures of socioeconomic change (see Kim, "Socio-Economic Development and Political Democracy in Japanese Prefectures," Choi, "Systems

Outputs, Social Environment, and Political Cleavages in Japan,"
and Benjamin et al., Patterns of Political Development. It is our
view that the variety of socioeconomic census measures typically
used in ecological analyses really tap the same basic underlying
dimension. One adds little explanatory power by adding several
more representative measures. Indeed, one runs into significant
multicollinearity problems; see Robert P. Althauser, "Multicollinearity and Non-additive Regression Models," in Herbert M.
Blalock, Jr., ed., Causal Models in the Social Sciences (Chicago:
Aldine-Atherton, 1971), pp. 453-72.

21. Our prefectural estimated koenkai membership figures
are based on a survey reported in Komei senkyo renmei [data
archives] (Tokyo).

4
FACTIONALISM IN
JAPANESE POLITICS

Factions are regarded by many commentators to be the real central force in Japanese politics. In order to understand the party system, one really needs to study how factions fit into it. Although the literature on factionalism is very large, confusion over the meaning of the concept, the assumptions underlying it, and the descriptions and explanations developed is just as large. Our goal here is to review and assess the literature on factionalism. The literature on Japanese factionalism is relatively well developed, so that arguments about factionalism encountered elsewhere are very likely to be present in the Japanese literature.[1]

This chapter is organized into four parts. First, the literature is summarized and criticisms are offered. Second, basic elements of a framework for the analysis of political change are discussed. Third, hypotheses, potentially useful to research, are then discussed. Finally, an application is presented.

THE LITERATURE

Every close student of Japanese politics has been forcibly struck by the dominance of factions in the political party process. It is not a new phenomenon: observers have noted its salience since the origin of political parties in the last decades of the nineteenth century.[2] We shall concentrate on the recent literature on the subject.

Though any summary makes for arbitrary categorizations, we found that the literature could be subsumed under three general divisions.[3] First are those works that present the general characteristics of the factions and factionalism. The intent is primarily descriptive. Numbers, size, and specific membership of the factions are presented.[4] For the most part, the discussions center on the House of Representatives, though Thayer has recently extended attention to the House of Councillors. Social background characteristics of various faction members, for example, educational background, age, generational differences, occupational patterns, and interest group connections are examined in the attempt to provide classifications based on one or more of these factors.[5] Some studies contain biographical information on specific faction leaders.[6] One of the central questions approached in this manner concerns which factions contain more ex-bureaucrats versus career politicians. In the same descriptive category are the more or less brief histories of postwar factionalism.

The second division of literature is comprised of those works that deal with Japanese factionalism in terms of different sorts of causal explanations. The cultural patterns of oyabun-kobun relationships, obligations and loyalty, and familial behavior patterns are cited as providing deep-seated models for interaction that predispose the Japanese to a factional style of politics.[7] In historical terms, the continuity of current factionalism with the prewar variety is stressed, as well as postwar developments, such as the purge of party leaders by the U.S. Occupation authorities. The structure of the Japanese party system is given the most weight in attempts to account for Japanese factionalism. The factors emphasized are the multimember district electoral system,* the method of selecting the party head (especially in the case of the LDP),[8] financial requirements for individual candidates, and the conflict between ex-bureaucrats and career politicians.[9] Factionalism provides an outlet for ideological distinctions among members of the larger political party.[10] It may be caused by the struggle for political rewards, for example, party executive and ministerial posts.[11] Psychologically, it may be a result of the need for identification with a group.[12]

In the third category are works that deal with the consequences of results of the Japanese factional system, offering both analytic and evaluative judgments. Analytically, factionalism is held to control political leadership change and recruitment in Japan and to determine communication of information between the faction leaders and the

---

*Everyone considers the electoral district structure an important determinant. In all but one electoral district, from three to five representatives are elected to the House of Representatives, though each voter casts a single ballot and representation is decided by plurality.

rank and file, including organizational and financial aid.[13] Factionalism within the LDP may be seen as a substitute for interparty
competition,[14] and thus as having an impact on public policy making.[15]

Evaluatively, students have concluded that factionalism in-
hibits the growth of political party responsibility,[16] prevents the
growth of local community political party organization,[17] and pro-
motes or contributes directly to political corruption. It also prevents the selection of national political leaders based on ability or
expertise in public policy making.

Three works require particular comment. Scalapino and
Masumi made one of the first attempts to organize biographical
data on Diet members and relate it to the composition of the factions. They themselves indicate, though, that their data are sug-
gestive rather than definitive. Totten and Kawakami were the first
to attempt to provide a theoretical framework with which to account
for Japanese factionalism. Their approach analyzes factionalism in
terms of the functions it performs. For example, they argue that
factions perform the functions of party leadership selection, financial support, and interelite competition itself. Functional theory,
however, leaves a good deal to be desired in general,[18] and its use
for the explanation of factionalism also brings forth specific problems. Which one among the functions performed by factionalism is
the most important? Perhaps all other functions are a consequence
of, for example, the structural method of electing the party president. Logically, one is unable to sort this out by using the functional approach. A related problem is that we are never certain
whether all, some, or one of the functions listed as being performed
by factionalism are necessary and/or sufficient. A functional explanation of factionalism would be useful if we were able to state the
boundary conditions delimiting the forces that affect it. As it now
stands, though, we do not know whether or not the form and content
of the political party system itself is (to use the language) a function
of something else, for example, the peculiar Japanese penchant for
group-consensus-oriented decision making. Leiserson's work is an
extraordinarily successful effort to utilize an important problem
area, such as functionalism within the LDP, to critically evaluate
and revise game theoretical approaches to the problem of coalition
formation. As such, it is primarily a work in political theory rather
than an effort to describe and explain the causes of factionalism.

A CRITIQUE

The assumptions underlying the critical remarks that follow
deviate to some extent from those underlying the work criticized.

While we, as well as other students of Japanese factionalism, are interested in furthering understanding concerning the substance of the process in terms of description of the actors in the process, factional realignments, and so forth, we are also committed to basic aspects of the value system of science as they apply to political analysis. This means we would seek to build a theoretical framework to account for factionalism from which one could develop operational definitions and, hence, hypotheses that could be empirically tested. It is only through this approach that we can, albeit imperfectly, develop generalizations that form a basis for cumulative knowledge about the subject. Value judgments are inescapable in political inquiry—as, for example, the value choice we have just outlined concerning the utility of the value system of science. These value judgments are vital in the initial problem selection. It is here that the investigator of Japanese politics decides whether or not to choose factionalism as his/her central focus over, say, voting behavior.* At a minimum, however, the investigator retains the responsibility to make his/her value statements explicit. He/she must attempt to separate value judgments from analytic statements when making his/her analysis.

Our critical discussion that follows is based on examination of the literature and the employment of our process view of Japanese political change.

The most general problem concerns how the concept of faction is treated. There are two general methods applicable to conceptual delimitation. A priori, the investigator may state that x is defined in terms of y and z. He/she then looks for the presence or absence of y or z. Alternatively, he/she may inductively allow the concept to emerge through a full description of clusters of similar attributes. This last method is that taken by students of factionalism. Definitions of factionalism consist of lists of characteristics.

Quantitatively, we suppose a faction is a relatively small group of individuals linked together by some set of incentive and/or sanctions for the purpose of attaining and maintaining political leadership. Among the studies reviewed, Johnston offers a representative definition. He defines factionalism as a "system of leadership-followership in which a high degree of importance is placed within a

---

*Values enter at the evidence acceptance or rejection stage as well. Only the scholar can determine whether there is sufficient evidence for the generalizations he/she makes. He/she must do so in light of the seriousness of the error possibility if the evidence is wrong or insufficient. If his/her concepts and evidence are replicatable, others may dispute his/her value judgments.

party system, or some significant part of it, on permanent or semi-permanent relationships involving substantial personal ties, which may also be formalized in some kind of institutional mold."[19] Johnston's definition is sufficiently general as to allow comparative analysis (which he himself undertakes). It is clear, for example, that small groups, that is, factions, control the activities of political parties in Western democracies.[20] What is wanted is an approach that links the concept factionalism with a larger comparative framework. This we attempt to do in the section, "Toward a Model of Factionalism."

Another point on the term itself concerns the pejorative connotations it brings forth. Factions are divisive, the opposite of the high-minded pursuit of ideals in the political world; James Madison's Federalist Paper number 10 remains a classic attack on the evils of factionalism. Employment of the term itself inclines all concerned toward its negative consequences and therefore prevents full and accurate description and explanation of the phenomena as one set of political behaviors in the political process. For example, political leadership recruitment is typically seen as the characteristic of factionalism in Japanese politics or as a function performed by it. Generally, this is criticized because it is undemocratic or politically irresponsible, that is, a small number of men in the LDP pick the key political leaders for Japan.[21] Two observations, though, come to mind. We know of no political system where small groups do not dominate the national political leadership process. This is the case in the Western democracies and, if recent work is to be believed, the case in Communist systems as well. Of course, in competitive political party systems, excessive attention to the private incentive systems of one or another faction is curtailed by the presence of others eager to capitalize on weaknesses shown by the opposition. Still, the number of competitive political party systems is small;* thus, surely the kind of political recruitment system in Japan is not an exceptional case.

We have comments on other points as well. First, factionalism is apparently often taken as being isomorphic with Japanese politics itself. But this is not the case; descriptions of the moves and countermoves of groups called factions are not sufficient explanations of the central problems in Japanese politics. The study of factionalism must be connected with more general issues, such as

---

*Though any definition of competitiveness is arbitrary, the presence of political parties in opposition with support from roughly 40 percent of the electorate suffices. Outside of Japan, only the Western European and Anglo-American countries qualify.

political party organization, political participation, or political leadership. Second, the prediction, hope, or demand that factions will disappear recurs throughout the literature. They are based on statements by political leaders that factionalism must die,[22] on the feeling that political participation is becoming increasingly related to political parties as autonomous entities rather than to individuals, and on the notion that the requirements of ongoing industrialization will inevitably render factionalism obsolete. There is little evidence, however, one way or another that the political parties are becoming more legitimate or autonomous in Japan. Main current faction leaders who state that factionalism is bad and must be eliminated simply reflect their agreement with the negative connotation associated with the term. There is little new in this; intellectuals everywhere have been captured by the rhetoric of democratic thought. Just as no political leaders anywhere are opposed to democracy, no Japanese political leader is opposed in principle to the elimination of factionalism and the broadening of political party responsibility. Finally, the modernization thesis is a variant of the convergence thesis, which pervades most of the literature on the development process in Japan. This view holds that the functional requirements of industrialization inevitably lead to congruence of the social, economic, and political processes of the societies that have passed through the basic stages of industrialization. In the case of Japanese factionalism, we have waited since the 1890s.

A last criticism concerns data problems—specifically, the methods and techniques of investigation used. Major data sources are newspaper and magazine accounts, party and factional publications, and nonfocused interviews with Diet members. There is nothing wrong with these sources if they are related to meaningful theoretical frameworks. With the exceptions of Scalapino and Masumi and Leiserson, however, data contained are illustrative. Thus, the thrust of present efforts is largely historical-descriptive, and there is little accumulation of knowledge about factionalism. We would point out that although sampling techniques are difficult to apply to Diet members, other potentially relevant methodologies include participant-observation, sociometric techniques,[23] and small groups analysis, which could be used to test generalizations about factionalism.

FACTIONALISM AND POLITICAL CHANGE

On balance, we think the most serious problem of this approach is the absence of theory in the analysis of Japanese factions. We do not suggest we have such a theory, but the political change approach that follows is offered as a structuring principle for relating studies of factions to political party institutionalization work. Our view of the political change process keys on the tripartite relationship between the process of community formation at the national level, the form of political participation, and governmental institutionalization. These dimensions are seen as being triggered by industrialization. It is not our concern to deal with the initial causal factors of industrialization. Nor are we concerned with dating it. We are interested in the politics of societies that have entered the industrial era in general and the Japanese case in particular. We do not assume that Japan began to march toward democratization or political stability. We do assume that industrialization and its concomitants have the effect of qualitative change on the existing social, economic, and political structures. Obviously, the distinctions we make here are analytic rather than concrete, and while we remain concerned only with the process of political change, the total developmental fabric is in reality intertwined. To stress our point, we refer only to the process of political change[24] when talking about the politics of societies that have entered the industrial age. We do this because it is our view that this term avoids the teleological consequences of much of the vocabulary social scientists use when talking about the process, a vocabulary that subtly affects the images of the development phenomenon itself. Political change process refers only to a problem area and nothing more.

Three dimensions are useful bases that encompass the key aspects of the political change process. We shall briefly articulate them in preparation for deriving some potential relationships with factionalism.

National Integration

Some students, following the pioneering work of Deutsch,[25] have identified the process of political community disintegration and reformulation at a more generalized level of complexity as a central ingredient in the political change process. The argument is as follows. Industrialization requires fundamental economic reorganization, reorganization at a much higher level of organized complexity. Functional specialization breeds further specialization, and capital requirements require large political entities within which to work. The village (and eventually the tribe) is too small a unit for this. Much larger population and geographic units become necessary—and, hence, larger political units. Then, too, growing urbanization, increased trade sponsored by a newly formed money economy, and increased regional migration contribute to a growing sense of common identity, language standardization, and the realization of, and acquiescence to, legitimate political authority previously restricted to the village or tribe. The nation is born.

This may be a very long historical process, and one that comes relatively early in the preindustrial period—or late and is thus encapsulated; the time allowed is very short in the current world.

This sketch covers the bare essentials of the process, but two qualifications must be added. First, even though the capital and the new nationally constituted central authority aspires to become the central legitimate and effective political authority, challenges may still be offered. For example, in retrospect, it is evident that the newly revised central political institutions were strong enough to defeat the disintegrative challenge afforded by the Satsuma Rebellion. However, there is nothing inevitable about any particular path to national integration. The combination of communities at a higher level of organization may be followed by the disintegration of these same organizations. The Prussians more or less successfully integrated the Rhineland, while the English apparently won over the Scots and the Welsh, but not the Irish. Many nation-states in sub-Saharan Africa remain legal fictions created by colonial authorities ruled by the first-generation African elites, a generation that either accedes or reacts to a primarily Western-built image of their continent.

The second qualification refers to the early existence of a nationally oriented Japanese citizenry. This was true of Japan, in comparison with other societies, because of the emperor system, cultural patterns oriented toward daimyo ("feudal lords") authority rather than the village, ethnic and language homogeneity, and geographical isolation. The Japanese had already attained a high level of national integration by early Meiji; the question then concerned the content and thrust of the national political institutions rather than their existence or nonexistence. National integration is not, then, to our mind the primary area to focus on in a discussion that hopes to link factionalism and political development. However, it clearly is a prerequisite for the other dimensions of political participation and governmental institutionalization and, thus, is ultimately important in such a discussion as this.

Political Participation

There is a growing consensus that mass political participation inevitably follows from industrialization. The existence of large numbers of former peasants in the capital alone supplies the opportunity for widening political participation. In the preindustrial period, there typically exists a wide gulf between the capital and the countryside due to problems of transportation, communication, and a simple barter economy, which removes the incentive for interaction between inhabitants of these two areas. The movement toward mass political participation may take many decades or, like national integration, may be compressed into only a few decades.*

Two aspects of political participation need to be considered. The first is the development of increased political participation itself, as seen in increased levels of voting, demonstrations, riots, awareness of issues, and so forth. Here, one is concerned with the social and economic changes that demonstrably lead to mass political participation. Second, why do societies differ greatly in the style and content of mass political participation? For example, Japan's rural social structure provided an important bulwark of political stability during a period (from approximately 1868 to 1927) when very rapid change was occurring. Although some scholars see political participation as a function of economic development, Deutsch's social mobilization concept[26] captures more accurately the intervening cultural and social forces that interact to produce increased political demands and, eventually, participation. No one has yet, however, systematically related the forms of political participation to the potential reactions available within the existing political structure at the time of rapidly increasing political participation. In the preindustrial society, the level of complexity of the "national" political organizations may be more or less rudimentary or highly developed, as in the case of the emperor system and the Tokugawa shogunate. Irrespective of the level of complexity of these political institutions, however, the Japanese did not engage in mass political participation. For us, it is the nexus between the political participation dimension and the pattern of growth and change of the central political institutions that is crucial to the study of the political change process in general and factionalism in Japan in particular. This is so because, as we shall attempt to argue in greater detail below, factionalism is one logical consequence of the combinatory process between political institutions, on the one hand, and the emerging pattern of political participation, on the other hand.

---

*Mass political participation may be defined as universal adult voting suffrage. Other types of political participation, such as demonstrations and riots, are equally, if not more, important, but equally difficult to measure.

Institutionalization

The relationship between the legitimacy and effectiveness of any set of central political institutions and the pursuit of the "best" or "good" political state is not new to any student of politics who has read classical political philosophy either of the Western or Eastern variety. Students of political change must deal with this problem in a specific context. As a result or as a concomitant of increased political participation following in the wake of sustained industrialization, the existing political institutions are changed substantially or, in a majority of cases, overthrown.

To analyze whatever type of political institutions that emerge after industrialization is quite another matter. What must be realized is that assumptions, unverified, even undefined, about the political change process are unavoidable. The choice of assumptions, however, is not thus less critical. A good deal of work on Japanese factionalism consciously or unconsciously accepts the assumption that representative political participation is an important element in government.

For us, the central focus is institutionalization. By this, we mean that political institutions may be studied as types of organizations. Organizations may be seen as structured sets of role patterns; hence, political institutions may be viewed as especially well delimited sets of role patterns. Specifically, a political institution consists of patterned behavior governed (ordered) by cultural norms specialized to the shaping and distribution of political values. Perhaps a crucial addition to this definition is the view that an institution is a "stably organized syndrome."[27] Political institutions may be thought of as the centrally defined (placed) control mechanisms for the political process. Through political institutions, legitimate force is employed or its threat made visible. The most distinctive political institution is the government, but other examples include political parties, interest groups, and a host of other routinized activities that may be developed from patterns of politically relevant culture traits, such as judicial review, seniority systems in legislatures, and, in Japan, factions.

Following Huntington's seminal work, much of the work on political change has focused on the existence of development of strong central institutions, along with our process assumption. We shall use this work as a point of departure. Basically, it is the task of particular political institutions to organize politics. In order to achieve this, mechanisms that both direct political participation and respond to it must be created. It is here where the "new" and "old" organization patterns become routinized and interfaced.

It is important to note that a political party is only one of the possible mechanisms for elite-mass linkage in Japan. While our focus is on how political party, faction, and koenkai relate to each other at different units and levels of analysis, we also call attention to the public bureaucracy, which clearly is a major political institution in the Japanese setting. In this chapter, we examine the relationship between political parties and factions at the national levels. Following that, we shall look at the way koenkai, the political party, and factions interrelate at the prefectural level. We emphasize the need to be alert to alternative institutionalized models that may perform apparent political-party-related functions, particularly as Japan moves into the postindustrial process-state.

TOWARD A MODEL OF FACTIONALISM

At the national level, it may be beneficial to view the Japanese party system, and its dominant feature of factionalism, in terms of its level or style of institutionalization. This would recognize, first of all, that political parties may be placed on a continuum that ranks party systems on the basis of such features as autonomy, complexity, and scope.[28] Autonomy refers to the inherent capacity of the political party organization itself to be differentiated from special interests. In Japan, there is a close relationship between political parties and special interests. Though it draws heavily on rural support, the LDP primarily represents the interests of Japanese business, particularly big business. It is acknowledged that big business provides this party and its factions with a great deal, if not almost all, of their campaign funds. By contrast, the Socialist Party speaks for labor. It primarily represents the interests of a single pressure group, Sohyo (General Council of Trade Unions of Japan). Like the Socialist Party, the Democratic Socialist Party has a single dominant base of support, Domei (Japanese Confederation of Labor). Komeito is the political arm of the Sokagakkai religious organization.

Complexity refers to the number and variety of roles in existence in the political party system. The number of tasks performed is itself a determinant of the number of roles, but is also a function of the role structure in existence. In Japan, the level of complexity of the party system is perhaps less than, say, that of Great Britain because (1) the factions perform some of the tasks allotted to the political parties in Great Britain, and (2) control of some basic aspects of political influence is held by the public bureaucracy.

Scope (or penetration) identifies the extent to which the political party extends to the local community level. This dimension is a basic key in the building of communication channels between the

public, the party, and the government. In Japan, there is little
political party organization at the local level. Organization units of
the LDP typically do not extend below the 47 prefecture headquarters,
and the Socialist parties are hardly better equipped with their own
local party organizations. Komeito, because of its overlapping
structure with Sokagakkai, does maintain a strong local organizational base; so does the Communist Party. In the case of the LDP,
koenkai have developed at the local level as political groups loyal to
individuals.

Using this view of institutionalization, one may differentiate
party systems along a continuum. One-party systems prevalent in
Africa, for example, would be at one end of the continuum, while
political party systems such as Great Britain and Sweden, which
enjoy a high degree of institutionalization, would be placed at the
other end. Figure 4.1 presents this point in an illustrative manner.
Apparently, Japan falls between the other systems.

FIGURE 4.1

Political Party Systems Compared by
Their Level of Institutionalization

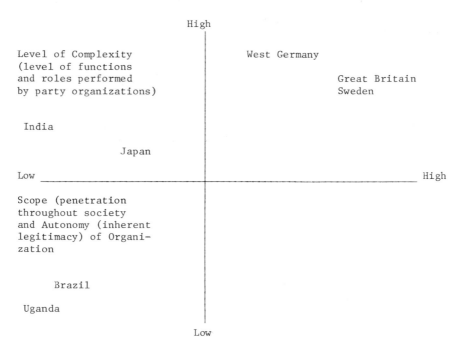

Source: Compiled by the authors.

One additional perspective to be subsumed under the institutionalization framework is that of recent work in organization theory.
Using the organizational perspective, the investigator must chart
the nature of the positive and/or negative sanctions available to the
faction leaders. This is based on recent work which suggests that
groups are cohesive and powerful in direct proportion to the sanctions available to an organization's leadership to entice or coerce
individual members of the group to comply with their wishes.

The level of institutionalization of the political party system
in general and the factional system in particular is determined by
the complex set of factors indicated in the relationships posited in
Figure 4.2. The remaining task is to present a conceptual model
that limits the aspects of the political, social, and economic environments (see Figure 4.2) that may be admitted for analysis.

FIGURE 4.2

Determinants of Factionalism

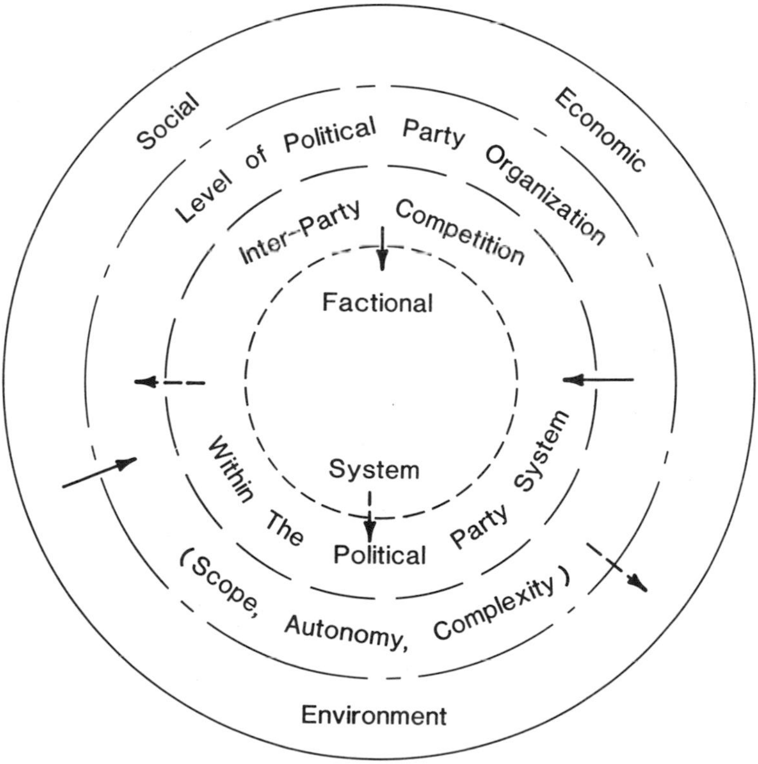

Source: Compiled by the authors.

There are four broad types of relationships that are assumed to affect factionalism in the Japanese political party process.

1. Within the LDP, which dominates the political party system in Japan, influence is exerted through small groups organized as factions. How are these groups organized, and what are the consequences of this organization?
2. The level of interparty competition between the larger LDP organization and the remaining parties is seen as a constraint on factional activity within the LDP.
3. The level of interparty competition and the level of factionalism may be related to the level of institutionalization of the political party organizations in the party system.
4. Finally, the political party system itself may be related to the development level of the socioeconomic environment.

Figure 4.2 illustrates these categories and the mutual interactive forces at work between them. In this scheme, the factional system is taken as the unit of analysis, with the other categories arranged in concentric circles around it in a manner that illustrates our belief that factionalism is determined by a multiple set of factors at different levels of analysis. We are not, we hasten to add, claiming that we are proposing a theory of factionalism. However, correct formulation of the arena within which to ask the theoretical questions is a needed step.

MAJOR CONCEPTS

Faction

Faction is defined as the primary unit of reference for individual members of the LDP (and the Socialist Party, and so forth). Political influence and its attached symbols, such as party and governmental offices, are distributed through the factions. Each faction is organized in terms of a leader with his followers. The leader's influence is maintained through operation of multiple factors, such as financial and political rewards at his disposal, personal loyalty of followers, and the group orientation of individual Diet members.

Political Party System

The political party system is the major vehicle for the exercise of political influence in the Japanese political process. Political parties are organizations with the primary purpose of attaining and maintaining the political leadership in the political process. A variety of other tasks may be performed, such as voter education and various internal organization activities. The level of institutionalization of the political party is determined by a number of factors, such as geography, social class stratification, and the configuration of the total economic and social environment[29]—relating, for instance, rural-urban migration, level and pace of economic development, social class mobility, interest group activity, and the party system's own performance in the exercise of political influence over time.

Influence

There are extraordinary difficulties attached to the operationalization of this concept, but we conceive of it as the end product in any two-person (in our case, a two-group, that is, faction) relationship. This may constitute an important problem for political inquiry. The size and cohesion of individual factions constitute the primary arena of evidence to assess whether faction a has more influence than faction b.

HYPOTHESES

The hypotheses that are presented are derived from the conceptual model. Whether or not the hypotheses are corroborated in the future is not the question here. For us, they represent important aspects of the problem to be systematically investigated. We stress the importance of juxtaposing our Japanese case with relevant theory sources.

Institutionalization Theory

From Huntington, Friedrich, Przeworski, and Sprague flow suggestions about the importance of the institutionalization of norms, values, and stable and enduring behavior patterns.[30]

Hypothesis 1: The closer the electoral system approaches the multiple-member district type, the greater the possibility factionalism will exist.

We have noted that Japan has a multiple-member (single-ballot) district electoral system. The greater the number of Diet members elected in a district (they range from one to five), the greater the possibility of candidates from the same political party and, hence, the greater the possibility of factionalism. This possibility derives purely from the nature of the electoral laws.[31]

Hypothesis 2: The higher the level of interparty competition, the lower the level of factionalism.

We simply assume here that the more equal the political parties are in competing for vote shares, the more dangerous intraparty competition will be. The greater the external threat the party organization faces, the greater the need for internal party organization and harmony. To the extent that patterns of interparty competition are institutionalized, factions within the parties will not become strong. In the absence of interparty competition, intraparty competition may act as a substitute in a party system dominated by one political party.

Hypothesis 3: The longer factionalism exists, the more institutionalized it becomes.

There are two senses in which this hypothesis is worthy of examination. It captures descriptively what has occurred in the Japanese instance. More importantly, institutional theory suggests that time is a key dimension for the institutionalization of any pattern of behavior. Expectations about the "correct" way to act, in this case, in a factional sense, usually solidify over a long period of time or in a short, compressed revolutionary experience. This suggests at least two research questions. Instead of asking about the factors that might account for the presence or continued existence of factionalism, we should also begin to look for factors which could possibly change it. In social research, this emphasis is known as the deviant case approach.

A recent failure in the Socialist Party provides an example. The Eda faction, relying on the "structural reform" theory, attempted to gain control of the party from 1960 to 1962. Eda attempted to deviate from the traditional factional machinery and appeal to the members at large. A careful examination of this attempt would be useful.[32]

Mobilization Theory

From Deutsch, Moore, and Lipset, we learn that it is the rate and sequence of social and economic change spurred by industrialization that is crucial.[33]

Hypothesis 4: The shorter the period available for industrialization, the greater the difficulties concerning the successful transplantation of new and foreign political institutions, such as political parties, and the greater the reliance on familiar (traditional) organizational models, such as factions.

The point here is that Japan essentially transformed its economy from primarily agrarian to predominantly industrial system in 30 years (1870 to 1900).

Political Culture

Hypothesis 5: The greater the tendency of the political culture to stress positive orientations toward the regime and political party identification, the lower the level of factionalism.

According to Almond and Verba, positive political orientations are associated with high levels of social and economic development, which in turn are related to the level of political party development.[34] In Japan, only the Communist Party and Komeito have developed solid local party organizations (see Table appendix). In the case of Komeito, the local party support organization appears to be isomorphic with Sokagakkai, the Nichiren-shoshu Buddhist sect.

Hypothesis 6: The greater the level of organizational complexity in preindustrial society, the greater the possibility that familiar organizational models, such as factions, will be used in the process of modernization and political change.

This hypothesis has several antecedents, which we note. First, as we note at several points in this book, we do not agree with the general argument often cited by Japan specialists that Japanese political behavior is unique because of tradition. Again, there can be no question that the cultural value systems implied by tradition describe important elements of political behavior. However, tradition cited as an explanation becomes completely tautological when students of Japanese politics argue essentially that the Japanese are the way they are because of their traditional value system, that is, they are Japanese. It is clear to us that tradition, used as a residual explanation category, is not very helpful in understanding Japanese politics. This does not mean we ignore the cultural value system. On the contrary, we assume that since Japan is the outstanding case of a non-European/Anglo-American society to move through the modernization process in an endogenous fashion, that familiar organizational models will continue to serve the Japanese unless they prove wholly incongruent with the requirements of modernization.[35]

Organization and Collective Goods Theory

Hypothesis 7: (1) The greater the number of positive incentives and negative sanctions commanded by a factional leader, the greater the number of members in his faction, and (2) the greater the number of positive incentives and negative sanctions wielded by the faction leaders, the higher the level of factionalism. Positive incentives include ministerial and other party posts, financial support for electoral campaigns, and organizational support for members of the factions. Negative sanctions include the withholding of positive incentives plus expulsion from the faction.

These two hypotheses flow from the work of Buchanan and Tullock; Olson; and Frolich, Oppenheimer, and Young, who have laid the groundwork for the application of the theory of collective goods to political organizations.[36]

Hypothesis 8: The higher the level of political party organization, the lower the level of factionalism.

This is a corollary of hypothesis 7 and is correct by definition, since factions may operate successfully only in the absence of party organization, which itself may be able to effect the incentives and sanctions outlined in hypothesis 7.

Hypothesis 9: The greater the tendency of nonpolitical party institutions (that is, the military, the bureaucracy, and possibly unions) to exert political influence, the higher the level of factionalism.

The hypothesis refers to the often cited equation between the exercise of political power and the development of responsible attitudes toward its use. Structurally, Japan has benefited from the existence of a strong, well-organized public bureaucracy, but this may very well have weakened the development of party organization.

SUMMARY

Our list of hypotheses is surely not exhaustive, but we hope it and the discussion preceding it have served its major purpose of widening the dialogue concerning factionalism in Japan politics. The task is to relate these, and other, hypotheses so as to assess their relative, as well as individual, importance as determinants of factionalism. For one conclusion, emerging with some clarity from our reading of the literature, is that single-factor explanations do not capture the richness of the problem in its total ramifications; a multivariate analysis is needed.

One comment concerns the need to connect analysis of factionalism with a major area of concern for democratic theory. While everyone is concerned with the process of factionalism and, to a lesser degree, its determinants, the consequences of the intraparty competition within the LDP on public policy have been largely ignored.[37] A prevailing view apparently has it that public policy determination is largely unrelated to internal competition within the LDP and that ministerial changes have little or no impact either. Observers of Japanese politics typically point to the public bureaucracy as being the "real" center of public policy making.[38] This may indeed be the case, but it must be corroborated. The finding that factionalism is, after all, not related to public policy formation would be of singular importance for comparative political theory. For it is an axiom of democratic theory that in political party systems, competition among political party elites is highly related to public policy outcomes.

Finally, what is the impact of postindustrialization on the factional system? With Japan's particular institutionalized arrangements—factions, parties, koenkai—interfaced with the public bureaucracy and large business organizations, will the rise in political participation and changing nature of political demands forecast or necessitate a wholesale set of changes? Or, as some suggest, is the Japanese political system and the factions within it, with its emphasis on consensus decision making, more equipped to meet the needs of a postindustrial age than other political systems?

AN APPLICATION: A MODEL OF FACTIONS WITHIN THE LIBERAL DEMOCRATIC PARTY

Let us see to what extent we can work with the hypotheses outlined under our "Organization and Collective Goods Theory" heading. If we view factions in Japanese politics as coalitions, we may employ the power of coalition theory to model their behavior. This would be a useful exercise, because coalition theory is based on our individual rational choice assumption from which, we argue, it is possible to derive nonobvious inferences about important elements of Japanese political behavior. The assumption of individual rationality is, of course, controversial, but we shall simply assert it here and wed it to a coalition model of factional behavior within the LDP. First, however, we must justify the treatment of factions as coalitions.

We have defined factionalism as a system of leadership-followership relationships that are reasonably stable across time. Moreover, within the Diet, the LDP is best understood as a series of factions or a factional system. These factions, we shall argue, are profitably understood as coalitions that individual LDP members join for a set of material benefits and protection from being isolated in an uncertain political world.

—————————————

This section is co-authored with William Morris.

We have divided the conditions that affect factional behavior into external and internal categories. From Table 2.5 (Results of General Elections for House of Representatives), we feel reasonably confident in our assumption—an important one for this analysis— that LDP factions have operated with moderate external constraints on their internal degree of competitiveness. In fact, we find evidence (Table 4.3) below which presents an amendment to the standard prediction that the LDP's demise is imminent; our characterization of the style and content of the external environment within which the LDP operates suggests that the LDP may continue to be very important for some time.

If external conditions do not emphasize a high degree of interparty competition and the strength of LDP organization remains weak (koenkai being the substitute), the internal incentives and sanctions for the maintenance of the factional system are what provide the basis for its strength. The incentives include: (1) financial aid for campaigns, (2) committee assignments, (3) attainment of cabinet rank, (4) important party posts and parliamentary vice-ministerships, and (5) the possibility of achieving these sorts of rewards in the future. These, then, are the assumptions that we argue faction leaders and members operate on.

A final argument to be examined concerns whether LDP intraparty factional competitiveness has declined over the last 20 years. If, as some observers argue, internal competitiveness has declined between the LDP factions, the argument for the use of coalition theory is weakened. As a check, we computed a fractionalization index based on an entropy index: far from declining over the period from 1958, the first election held after the LDP was formed in 1955, to 1977, the factional system within the LDP remained at least as competitive in 1977 as it was in the 1950s. (See Figure 4.3.)*

---

*To begin with, let us assume that entropy measures intraparty competition within the LDP and that this competition equals the amount of factionalism occurring at any given point in time. Thus, in this case, entropy (H) will be calculated:

$$H = \sum_{i=1}^{N} p_i \log_{10} p_i = \sum_{i=1}^{N} p_i \log \frac{1}{p_i} \times 3.32193$$

where p_i = percent of the total N in each faction with N factions existing at each time point. The higher the level of entropy, the higher the level of factionalism.

FIGURE 4.3

LDP Intraparty Entropy Index, 1958-76

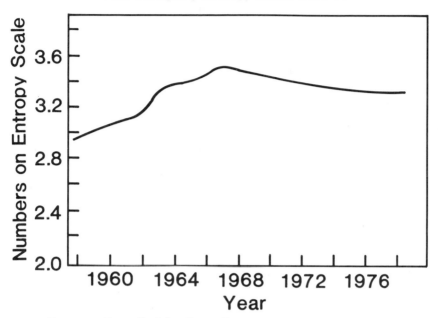

Source: Compiled by the authors.

A COALITION MODEL

A faction is an organizational structure through which like-minded representatives may secure goods for themselves. As was pointed out, these goods may take many forms: pork barrel, ideological victories, or personal status increase, either real or symbolic. But a truly multifactional system in which no faction is supreme ordinarily necessitates that these groups must deal with one another. In other words, factions must strive to form winning coalitions in order to partake in rewards.

Success in coalition formation, at first blush, would appear directly related to the size of the faction. Obviously, a larger faction would add more votes to a coalition than a smaller one and thus increase the group's chances for victory. But size as the sole factor fails to capture certain dynamics of the coalition building process. The percentages split among all factions may be such that different-sized groups may be equally effective. There is a clear need, then, to explicitly define factional effectiveness.

The treatment of factional effectiveness, or factional power, that follows borrows heavily from the Shapley-Shubik power index.[39] These two scholars defined their index as the probability that a faction will be pivotal in changing a losing coalition to a winning one when the final coalition is built upon a random selection of all the groups—that is, no coalition structure permitted within the rules of the legislature or party convention may be excluded for idiosyncratic reasons. They reasoned that the pivotal position was extremely important to rational actors because of the rewards that could be demanded for changing a losing to a winning coalition. At such a time, the players responsible for the conversion could demand the lion's share of the value of the victory. Admittedly, randomness is a rather strict assumption about the coalition building process; but a priori, the researcher is unable to predict the true deviation from randomness, and this assumption seems reasonable under those circumstances.

Perhaps an example would be helpful at this point. Consider a 110-member legislature composed of four political parties. No party has a straight majority, which will be taken as the necessary condition for victory; thus coalition building is necessary for the legislative process to continue. Suppose the parties possess the number of seats shown in Table 4.1. With this assumed distribution of seats, the following are all the possible winning coalitions, where the order of entry into the coalition is overlooked: (B,C), (B,D), (C,D), (A,B,C), (A,B,D), (B,C,D), (A,C,D), and (A,B,C,D).

TABLE 4.1

Example of Hypothetical Parliament

Party	Seats	Fraction of Seats	Power Index
A	10	1/11	0
B	30	3/11	1/3
C	30	3/11	1/3
D	40	4/11	1/3

Source: Compiled by the authors.

Looking in more detail at (B,C,D) will provide insight into the calculation process. The following six arrangements are assumed in that coalition: (B,C,D,A), (C,D,B,A), (D,B,C,A), (B,D,C,A), (C,B,D,A), and (D,C,B,A). By arrangement (B,C,D,A), it is meant that B is the founding member of the coalition, C then joins, and then D. In (B,C,D,A), party C is said to be pivotal, since prior to its membership, the coalition was losing (30 votes) and after incorporation, winning (60 votes). Each possible arrangement is then examined and the pivotal player identified. The number of pivots for each party is then divided by the number of possible arrangements—in this case, 24—to obtain the probability of each party playing the pivotal vote.

The results in the example are rather intriguing. Party A is powerless in the context of this legislature, since it never becomes the pivotal member of any coalition. So, although a party may possess a non-zero number of seats in a legislature, it may be strategically irrelevant to the legislative process. Also, although party D holds the greatest share of seats, it has no more power than the two parties that possess 25 percent less numerical strength. Hence, power defined in this fashion does not increase monotonically with party seats.

In order to calculate the power of a faction in the LDP membership of the Japanese Diet, either structural or political constraints placed upon the coalition process must be made explicit. In the example above, no contraints were necessary, since party interactions and special rules were not incorporated into the model. We note that ordinarily, the LDP president is elected by the party convention, which is held every two years. Because the party convention is controlled by the LDP Diet members—they constitute an overwhelming majority at the party conventions—the coalitions formed within the Diet membership may be used to predict the outcome of the party convention's presidential election.

A formula that summarizes the calculation process for faction i for the Shapley-Shubik power index is given by:

$$1_i = \sum_{i \ s} \frac{(s-1)! \ (n-s)!}{n!} \ [v(S) - v(S - \{i\})]$$

where s is the number of factions in coalition S and n is the number of factions in the "parliament"; v(S) refers to the value of the coalition formed and generally is defined to be equal to "one" if winning and "zero" if losing; $v(S - \{i\})$ is the value of the coalition S with faction i excluded. It should be obvious that the only coalitions that are relevant for the calculation are those in which faction i is pivotal.

Table 4.2 illustrates the use of the formula in determining the Shapley-Shubik power index for the hypothetical example.

TABLE 4.2

Calculation of Shapley-Shubik Power Index
Utilizing Formula for Party B

Pivotal Subset		Power Index
(B, C)	$\dfrac{(2 - 1)! \ (4 - 2)!}{4!}$	$\dfrac{2}{24}$
(B, D)	$\dfrac{(2 - 1)! \ (4 - 2)!}{4!}$	$\dfrac{2}{24}$
(B, A, C)	$\dfrac{(3 - 1)! \ (4 - 3)!}{4!}$	$\dfrac{2}{24}$
(B, A, D)	$\dfrac{(3 - 1)! \ (4 - 3)!}{4!}$	$\dfrac{2}{24}$
		$\dfrac{1}{3}$

Source: Compiled by the authors.

In Japan, during the period covered in the analysis, however, realism dictates that two caveats be stated: (1) large "bureaucratic factions" and large "parliamentary factions" may not coalesce,[40] and (2) smaller factions may become partners in either a "bureau-cratic"-based coalition or "parliamentary"-based coalition.*

The effects of these assumptions are to partition the factions into three sets: large bureaucratic, large parliamentary, and small groups. The latter may join any coalition; the former two may not

---

*The bureaucratic or parliamentary factional division is based on images of faction leaders commonly held by the public and jour-nalists and so reported. The actual composition of a "parliamen-tary" faction may indicate that a majority of its members may, in fact, not come from parliamentary (party career) background. The same point describes bureaucratic factions.

share membership in any formation. As will be demonstrated, these "rules of the game" have a substantial impact on the effectiveness of each faction in the "legislative" environment. For illustrative purposes, two (parliamentary sessions) years—1960 and 1964—are closely examined.

The LDP in 1960 was composed of eight well-defined factions, whose total membership included 265 individuals, 22 double memberships, and 12 independents. Table 4.3 details the breakdown in the Diet.

TABLE 4.3

Power of the Factions in the LDP Membership
in the 1960 Japanese Diet

Faction	Number of Seats	Percentage of Seats among All Factions	Power Index
Ikeda	49	18.5	33.3
Kishi	45	17.0	33.3
Sato	44	16.6	33.3
Fujiyama	26	9.8	0.0
Kono	32	12.1	0.0
Ōno	26	9.8	0.0
Miki/Matsumura	25	9.4	0.0
Ishii	18	6.3	0.0
Total	265	100.0	99.9*
Numbers needed to win	133		
Double members	22		
Independents	12		
Party total	299		

*Error due to rounding.
Source: Yomiuri Shimbun [Yomiuri newspaper] (Tokyo, 1960).

The Ikeda faction, the largest in the LDP, also provided the prime minister. The large bureaucratic groups are those led by Ikeda, Kishi, and Sato; the large parliamentary factions are those led by Fujiyama, Kono, Ōno, and Miki/Matsumura. The Ishii faction is considered here as a small hybrid containing elements of both the parliamentary and bureaucratic orientations. Immediately evident is the fact that the power indexes do not bear an extremely close relationship to the faction sizes.

The parliamentary group, although they total 41.1 percent of the LDP factional structure, do not hold any power at all. This is because together, even with the aid of the Ishii members, they cannot force a winning coalition. The Kono faction would need to add seven members in order to change its power index; the other factions would require even more new members to play a part in the coalition formation process.

The bureaucratic groups are in a much better position. Through combining, they can achieve the numbers necessary to win. In spite of the small difference in the percentage of seats controlled by each faction, their power indexes are identical. They are identical because only a three-member Ikeda-Kishi-Sato coalition is victorious, and the last member joining is always pivotal in two of the six possible arrangements. Thus, the bureaucrats in 1960 possessed a power monopoly in the LDP membership of the Diet—and, therefore, the party convention.

Perhaps the most counterintuitive result concerns the Ishii faction. Since the group is small and also a hybrid, expectations might have been that a crucial role could have been played in certain situations. This is just not the case. As shown earlier, the parliamentary groups cannot form a winning coalition; hence, if the Ishii faction is to be pivotal, it must be so in a bureaucratic coalition. But Ishii can never be pivotal: for that faction to change a losing to a winning coalition, it must do so as the third member— an impossibility given that the total votes of Ishii and any other two bureaucratic factions is less than 133. The Ishii group, then, is in a totally unviable position in the power machinations of the LDP.

Since 1962 provides a competitive framework in the LDP very similar to that of 1960, the factional structure of 1964 is used for comparative analysis here. In 1964, there were nine factions with no one group holding more than 20 percent of the party membership. Table 4.4 presents the factional breakdown of that year. The large bureaucratic factions will be defined as those of Ikeda and Sato; the large parliamentary factions, those of Kono, Miki, and Ōno. The smaller floating factions, then, are Fukuda's, Fujiyama's, Kawashima's, and Ishii's. The latter set may, under the structural rules announced earlier, coalesce with members of either of the two former sets.

The political environment of this "Diet" is most easily considered as two simultaneous "games" taking place. The bureaucratic factions wish to recruit enough of the smaller groups to obtain more than 143 votes (a simple majority), while the parliamentary factions engage in analogous behavior. The power index can be determined for members of each group in a manner exactly like that of the 1960 "Diet"; Table 4.4 also provides these calculations.

TABLE 4.4

Power of the Factions in the LDP Membership
in the 1964 Japanese Diet

Faction	Number of Seats	Percentage of Seats among All Factions	Power Index
Coalition Partners of Bureaucratic Factions			
Ikeda	49	17.2	30.0
Sato	46	16.1	30.0
Fukuda	21	7.4	10.0
Fujiyama	21	7.4	10.0
Kawashima	19	6.7	10.0
Ishii	14	4.9	10.0
Coalition Partners of Parliamentary Factions			
Kono	48	16.8	34.6
Miki	37	13.0	11.3
Ono	30	10.5	11.3
Fukuda	21	7.4	10.7
Fujiyama	21	7.4	10.7
Kawashima	19	6.7	10.7
Ishii	14	4.9	10.7

Source: Kokkai Binran [Diet Handbook] (Tokyo: Nihon seikei chinbunsha, 1964-65).

Given that distribution of seats, the smaller factions should be fairly indifferent about which coalition they would join. The power index is approximately the same for both sets of possible partners. Each smaller faction's probability of becoming the pivotal member of the final winning coalition is approximately the same under both scenarios. This result is by no means generalizable to all conceivable "Diet" faction compositions; it is, rather, a peculiarity of the 1964 Diet.

An interesting result in the analysis of the parliament-based partners concerns the Kono faction. Due to the strengths of their possible coalition mates, the 25 percent edge that the Kono group has over the Miki group translates into a 200 percent gain on the power index. The reason for this jump is that the Kono faction is decisive for any winning coalition; that is, without Kono, the parliamentary factions cannot forge a victorious coalition.

It also should be noted that the power index is not zero for any faction in 1964. The possibility exists that even though a faction increases its seats in the Diet, there will be no increase in the strategic importance of the group. Likewise, change external to a faction might cause an abrupt increase or decrease in the power index even though their share of the seats remains invariant. These facts might account for the breaking apart of factions that were actually increasing in numerical strength: rational faction members would see their dilemma and act to increase their own individual power even at the expense of the unit.

CONCLUSION

We utilized a definition of power that rigorously follows from certain assumptions about rationality and coalition building. Those assumptions directly led to a formal unambiguous means of gauging factional effectiveness; other assumptions about the behavior modeled would have quite possibly resulted in a different analysis and conclusions about the Japanese "Diet." However, we feel our conclusions have been "validated" by impressionistic analyses of first-hand observers of the process who are undoubtedly not fluent in social choice models. In one sense, the formalization of the coalition process here may be seen as an attempt to clearly specify the mechanics so aptly reported by journalists.

Of course, there is always room for confusion and controversy over approaches in social inquiry, especially with respect to epistemological questions. However, if the goal is comparative theory development in the study of factions, which clearly form a large portion of political behavior, we offer the approach presented here as a fruitful strategy.

NOTES

1. A survey by the authors indicates that the concept of factionalism is present in virtually every country whose literature we examined. However, students of Indian politics are the other large group to focus on factionalism comparable to Japanese politics specialists. For example, see Paul Brass, Factional Politics in an Indian State: The Congress Party in Uttar Pradesh (Berkeley and Los Angeles: University of California Press, 1965); Ralph Nicholas, "Village Factions and Political Parties in Rural West Bengal," Journal of Commonwealth Political Studies 2 (November 1963): 17-32; and B. D. Graham, "The Succession of Factional Systems in the Uttar

Pradesh Congress Party, 1937-66," in Marc J. Swartz, ed., Local-Level Politics (Chicago: Aldine, 1968), pp. 323-60. Compare Carl Lande, Leaders, Factions and Parties: The Structure of Philippine Politics, Southeast Asian Studies, Monograph Series, no. 6 (New Haven, Conn.: Yale University Press, 1965).

2. For example, see Junnosuke Masumi, Nihon seitoshi-ron [A history of Japanese political parties], vols. 1-4 (Tokyo: Tokyo University Press, 1965-68); compare Nobutake Ike, The Beginning of Political Democracy in Japan (Baltimore, Md.: Johns Hopkins Press, 1950).

3. The following articles and volumes constitute the literature in English we consulted: Hans H. Baerwald, "Factional Politics in Japan," Current History 46 (April 1964): 223-29, 243-44; Hans H. Baerwald, "Japan at Election Time," Asian Survey 5 (January 1968): 640-55; Allan B. Cole, George O. Totten, and Cecil R. Uyehara, Socialist Parties in Postwar Japan (New Haven, Conn.: Yale University Press, 1966), chap. 9; Lee W. Farnsworth, "Challenges to Factionalism in Japan's Liberal Democratic Party," Asian Survey 6 (September 1966): 501-9; Lee W. Farnsworth, "Social and Political Sources of Political Fragmentation in Japan," Journal of Politics 29 (May 1967): 287-301; Haruhiro Fukui, "The Associational Basis of Decision-Making in the Liberal Democratic Party," in Papers on Modern Japan (Canberra, Australia: Research School of Pacific Studies, Institute of Advanced Studies, 1965), pp. 18-33; Haruhiro Fukui, Party in Power (Berkeley: University of California Press, 1970); Haruhiro Fukui, "Factionalism in a Dominant Party System: The Case of Japan," in Frank P. Belloni and Dennis C. Beller, eds., Faction Politics (Santa Barbara, Calif.: ABC-Clio Press, 1978); Scott D. Johnston, "A Comparative Study of Intra-Party Factionalism in Israel and Japan," The Western Political Science Quarterly 20 (June 1967): 288-307; H. Kamo, "Empirical Studies of the JSP Factions," Monograph Series, no. 5 (Tokyo: Japan Institute of Political Studies, 1975); Frank C. Langdon, "The Political Contributions of Big Business in Japan," Asian Survey 3 (October 1963): 465-73; Frank C. Langdon, "Japanese Liberal Democratic Factional Discord on China Policy," Pacific Affairs 41 (Fall 1968): 403-15; Frank C. Langdon, Politics in Japan (Boston: Little, Brown, 1967), chap. 5; Michael Leiserson, "Factions and Coalitions in One-Party Japan: An Interpretation Based on the Theory of Games," American Political Science Review 62 (September 1968): 770-87; Junnosuke Masumi, "A Profile of the Japanese Conservative Party," Asian Survey 3 (August 1963): 390-401; Robert A. Scalapino and Junnosuke Masumi, Parties and Politics in Contemporary Japan (Berkeley and Los Angeles: University of California Press, 1962), chaps. 3 and 5; James R. Soukup, "Japan, Comparative Political Finance: A Sym-

posium," Journal of Politics 25 (August 1963): 737-56; J. A. Stock-
win, "Factions and Ideology in Postwar Japanese Socialism," Papers
on Modern Japan (Canberra, Australia: Research School of Pacific
Studies, Institute of Advanced Studies, 1965), pp. 34-49; Koji
Sugimori, "Social Background of Political Leadership in Japan,"
The Developing Economies 6 (December 1968): 34-59; N. B. Thayer,
How the Conservatives Rule Japan (Princeton, N.J.: Princeton
University Press, 1969), chap. 2; George O. Totten and Tamio
Kawakami, "The Functions of Factionalism in Japanese Politics,"
Pacific Affairs 38 (Summer 1965): 105-22; George O. Totten, "Re-
cent Factional Developments in the Japan Socialist Party: The Rise
of New Types of Factions" (Paper presented at the annual meeting
of the International Studies Association, Toronto, Canada, February
1976).

　　In Japanese, we examined the following: Haruhiro Fukui,
Jiyuminshutō to seisaku-kettei [The Liberal Democratic Party and
policy-making] (Tokyo: Fukumura Shuppan, 1969), chap. 5;
Junnosuke Masumi, "Jiyuminshutō no soshiki to kinō" [Organization
and functions of the Liberal Democratic Party], in Japanese Politi-
cal Science Association, ed., Gendai nihon no seitō to kanryō [The
parties and bureaucracy in contemporary Japan] (Tokyo: Iwanami
Shoten, 1967), pp. 34-77; Kinichi Higuchi, "Senkyo, Seitō, habatsu"
[Elections, political parties and factions], in Dōshisha hōgaku
[Dōshisha law review] 12 (1961): 41-71; and Tamio Kawakami,
"Habatsu rikigaku ni tsuiteno ichi Kōsatsu" [The mechanism of fac-
tions in Japanese political parties: an analysis], Kōdōkagaku Kenkyu
[Behavioral science research] 2 (1966): 29-36. We note that all of
the above-mentioned authors except Higuchi have also written on
Japanese factionalism in English. There are three other scholarly
works on party factionalism available in Japanese in recent years,
all of which are translations from English works cited above:
Scalapino and Masumi, Gendai nihon no seitō to seiji (Tokyo: Iwanami
Shoten, 1962); Thayer (translated by Katsumi Kobayashi) Jimintō
[The Liberal Democratic Party] (Tokyo: Sekkasha, 1968); and a popular version of Leiserson's article, "Jiminto Towa Renritsu-Seiken
to Mitsuketari" [We found the Liberal Democratic Party to be a
coalition government], Chūō Kōron (August 1967): 188-201.

　　There is a dearth of scholarly work on the subject in Japanese.
Most Japanese writing on factionalism is produced by journalists.
Recent representative examples are the following: Asahi Shimbun,
ed., Seitō to habatsu [Political parties and factions] (Tokyo: Asahi
Shimbunsha, 1968); Yomirui Shimbun, ed., Seitō: Sono Soshiki to
Habatsu no Jittai [Political parties: their organizations and factional
realities] (Tokyo: Yomiuri Shimbunsha, 1966); and Tsuneo Watanabe,
Habatsu to tatōkajidai [Factionalism and an era of the multiparty

trend] (Tokyo: Sekkasha, 1967). Watanabe is worthy of note, as his pioneering work on the subject, Habatsu: hoshutō no kaibō [Factionalism: an analysis of the Conservative Party] (Tokyo: Kōbundō, 1958), was instrumental in promoting Western scholars' studies on factionalism. Another book by Watanabe on factionalism is Tōshu to seitō [Party president and political parties] (Tokyo: Kōbundō, 1961). Other journal articles on factionalism appear in such popular weekly and monthly magazines as Asahi janaru [Asahi journal], Chūō Kōron [The central review], Keizai-hyōron [Economic critique], Nihon no Ugoki [The movement in Japan], Sekai [World], Shisō [Thoughts], and Ushio [Tide].

4. See especially Baerwald, "Factional Politics in Japan"; Hans H. Baerwald, "Japan: The Politics of Transition," Asian Survey 4 (January 1968): 646-55; Hans H. Baerwald, "Japan: 'Black Mist' and Pre-Electioneering," Asian Survey 7 (January 1967): 31-39; and Baerwald, "Japan at Election Time"; Thayer, How the Conservatives Rule Japan; Fukui, Jiyuminshutō to seisaku-kettei; and Cole, Totten, and Uyehara, Socialist Parties in Postwar Japan.

5. Baerwald, "Factional Politics in Japan"; Baerwald, "Japan: The Politics of Transition"; Baerwald, "Japan: 'Black Mist' and Pre-Electioneering"; Baerwald, "Japan at Election Time"; Scalapino and Masumi, Parties and Politics in Contemporary Japan; Fukui, Jiyuminshutō to seisaku-kettei; and Kawakami, "Habatsu rekigaku ni tsuiteno ichi Kōsatsu."

6. Cole, Totten, and Uyehara, Socialist Parties in Postwar Japan, and Fukui, Jiyuminshutō to seisaku-kettai.

7. Farnsworth, "Challenges to Factionalism"; Totten and Kawakami, "Functions of Factionalism in Japanese Politics"; Scalapino and Masumi, Politics and Parties in Contemporary Japan; and Kawakami, "Habatsu rikigaku ni tsuiteno ichi Kōsatsu."

8. In particular, see Thayer, How the Conservatives Rule Japan.

9. Especially see Scalapino and Masumi, Parties and Politics in Contemporary Japan.

10. For example, Stockwin, "Factions and Ideologies in Postwar Japanese Socialism"; Totten and Kawakami, "Functions of Factionalism in Japanese Politics"; Kawakami, "Kabatsu rikigaku ni tsuiteno ichi Kōsatsu"; and Totten, "Recent Factional Developments in Japan Socialist Party."

11. Particularly Baerwald, "Factional Politics in Japan"; Baerwald, "Japan: The Politics of Transition"; Baerwald, "Japan: 'Black Mist' and Pre-Electioneering"; Baerwald, "Japan at Election Time" Fukui, Jiyuminshutō to seisaku-kettei; and Masumi, "Jiyuminshutō no soshiko to kino."

12. Thayer, How the Conservatives Rule Japan.

13. Totten and Kawakami, "Functions of Factionalism in Japanese Politics," and Fukui, Jiyuminshutō to seisaku-kettei.

14. Scalapino and Masumi, Politics and Parties in Contemporary Japan, and Masumi, "Jiyuminshutō no shoshiko to kinō."

15. See Fukui, Jiyuminshutō to seisaku-kettai, and Masumi, "Jiyuminshutō no soshiko to kinō."

16. For instance, Farnsworth, "Challenges to Factionalism in Japan's Liberal Democratic Party."

17. Masumi, "Profile of Japanese Conservative Party."

18. The literature on structural-functional analysis is vast. The most developed recent statement of its use in political science by its major proponent is in Gabriel Almond and G. Bingam Powell, Comparative Politics: A Developmental Approach (Boston: Little, Brown, 1967). The most penetrating critique of functional theory remains that by Carl G. Hempel, "The Logic of Functional Analysis," in Llewellyn Gross, ed., Symposium on Sociological Theory (Evanston, Ill.: Row, Peterson, 1959), pp. 207-307.

19. See Johnston, "Comparative Study of Intra-Party Factionalism in Israel and Japan"; Scalapino and Masumi, Parties and Politics in Contemporary Japan; and Kawakami, "Habatsu rikigaku ni tsuiteno ichi kōsatsu."

20. Robert Michels, Political Parties (New York: Collier Books, 1962); Frank Belloni, ed., Factions and Parties (Santa Barbara, Calif.: ABC-Clio Press, 1978).

21. Explicit exceptions are Totten and Kawakami, "Functions of Factionalism in Japanese Politics," and Thayer, How the Conservatives Rule Japan.

22. Jiyuminshuto (Liberal Democratic Party), Soshiki chōsaki tōshin (Tokyo: Jiyuminshuto, January 1963).

23. For a tentative and crude application of the sociometric techniques, see Higuchi, "Senkyo, Seitō, habatsu."

24. This has to do with assumptions regarding the direction of the political development process. The best statement on this is by Samuel P. Huntington, "Political Development and Political Decay," World Politics 17 (April 1965): 386-411. See also Roger W. Benjamin et al., Patterns of Political Development: Japan, India, Israel (New York: David McKay, 1972), pp. 1-28.

25. Karl W. Deutsch, Nationalism and Social Communication (Cambridge, Mass.: M.I.T. Press, 1966).

26. Karl W. Deutsch, "Social Mobilization and Political Development," American Political Science Review 55 (September 1961): 493-514.

27. For the ideas included in this section, see Benjamin et al., Patterns of Political Development, pp. 23-28, 30-41.

28. We borrow most heavily from Huntington, "Political Development and Political Decay"; for other attempts to utilize the institutionalization framework, see Nelson W. Polsby, "The Institutionalization of the United States House of Representatives," American Political Science Review 62 (March 1968): 148-68; Robert O. Keohane, "Institutionalization in the United Nations' General Assembly," International Organizations 23 (Autumn 1969): 859-96.

29. Frank J. Sorauf, Political Parties in the American System (Boston: Little, Brown, 1964). For the type of measures useful for relating the economic and social factors to an important political problem, see Roger W. Benjamin and John H. Kautsky, "Communism and Economic Development," American Political Science Review 62 (March 1968): 131-44.

30. Carl J. Friedrich, Man and His Government: An Empirical Theory of Politics (New York: McGraw-Hill, 1963), p. 71; Samuel P. Huntington, Political Order in Changing Societies (New Haven, Conn.: Yale University Press, 1968); Adam Przeworski and John Sprague, "Concepts in Search of Explicit Formulation: A Study in Measurement," Midwest Journal of Political Science 15 (May 1971): 183-218.

31. Douglas W. Rae, Jr., The Political Consequences of Electoral Laws (New Haven, Conn.: Yale University Press, 1971).

32. Kawakami, "Habatsu rikigaku nitsuiteno ichi kōsatsu." In this conjunction, recent activities of Shakai shugi-Kyokai (Socialism Association) and of anti-Kyokai groups are instructive as well.

33. Barrington Moore, The Social Origins of Democracy and Dictatorship (Boston: Beacon Press, 1966); S. M. Lipset, Political Man (New York: Doubleday, 1961); Deutsch, "Social Mobilization and Political Development."

34. Gabriel Almond and Sidney Verba, The Civic Culture (Princeton, N.J.: Princeton University Press, 1963). By political culture, Almond and Verba point to basic cultural patterns specifically directed toward the political subject.

35. For an excellent discussion of the role of tradition, see James W. White, "Tradition and Politics in Studies of Contemporary Japan," World Politics 26 (April 1974): 400-27.

36. Mancur Olson, Jr., The Logic of Collective Action (Cambridge, Mass.: Harvard University Press, 1965); and Norman Frolich, Joe Oppenheimer, and Oran Young, Political Leadership and Collective Goods (Princeton, N.J.: Princeton University Press, 1971).

37. Fukui, in Jiyuminshutō to seisaku-kettei, alludes to only the general negative consequences of factionalism on correct policy making.

38. T. J. Pempel, "The Bureaucratization of Policymaking in Postwar Japan," American Journal of Political Science 18 (November 1974): 647-64.

39. M. D. Davis, Game Theory (New York: Basic Books, 1970).

40. See Hans H. Baerwald, "Japan: New Diplomatic Horizons, Old-Style Domestic Politics," Asian Survey 8 (January 1968): 43-51; Baerwald, "Japan at Election Time"; Baerwald, "Factional Politics in Japan," pp. 223-29, 243-44.

5
KOENKAI: ELECTORAL
SUPPORT ORGANIZATIONS

INTRODUCTION

If factions are the central endogenous organizations relevant
to Japanese politics, koenkai comprise the second major organizational form. The basic question concerns whether organizational
forms of elite-mass linkage comprise a developmental progression
from candidate-oriented personal support organizations and factions,
as the locus of effective organization, to political party. Specifically, we will study the way koenkai (personal support organizations)
and political parties relate in the Japanese political change process.
Koenkai and political parties coexist in the political process. The
conclusion is reached that the view that there is a positive relationship between sociopolitical change and the development progression
noted is mistaken and must be revised at least with respect to the
Japanese case. In order to reach this conclusion, three steps are
taken: (1) the two theory sources—from the political development
and collective goods literature—which offer support for either side
of the structuring question are posed; (2) the concepts, units of
analysis, and measurement procedures are identified; and (3) the
findings are presented.*

----

*We note two caveats: (1) the study does not address or nec-
essarily diminish the significance of factions at the national level,
or the need for political parties in a parliamentary system; and
(2) the data are based on perceptions of legislators, not voters,
about what got legislators elected.

Theory Sources

The inference drawn from the political development literature is that we should expect an organizational progression; the reverse inference may be drawn from the collective goods approach. For those who work within the paradigm of the political development literature and focus on the Japanese case, the dilemma is the apparent gap between image and reality. Japan is a mature postindustrial society by any set of aggregate measures, and yet, while they agree that Japan is advanced socially and economically, observers do not agree that Japan has achieved a similar level of political development. For while the political party system frames political activity, factions and the public bureaucracies supported by business interests appear to be at the heart of Japanese politics. Since political development for many still means the growth and eventual institutionalization of a political party system, does this not mean that Japan lags behind other societies politically?[1]

However, from the collective goods theory, a different approach to the subject, the reverse argument may be supported. We note (Chapter 6) that while proponents of the collective goods approach would agree with the thoughtful critiques that question the explanatory status of cultural descriptions of Japanese social and political behavior,[2] these efforts would be accepted as more or less accurate descriptions of extant attitudes, values, and behaviors. We have also argued that from the perspective of individual rational choice, it is reasonable to expect endogenous organizational models to endure—even prosper—under conditions no longer supportive of them. From the collective goods theory, one would not treat organizational models such as koenkai as traditional residues doomed in the face of continuing sociopolitical change; rather, one would infer that such models will be adopted whenever possible to cope with the change-induced agent, in this case, the sociopolitical change beginning with the Meiji Restoration (1868).

RESEARCH DESIGN

First, we define our central concepts, koenkai, factions, and political parties. Political parties are distinguished from factions and koenkai by their ideological and structural characteristics. Political parties, if they are successful, become reference points for large components of individual and group activity in the political process, for example, nomination, financial support, and electoral support itself. Factions (habatsu) are relatively small groups of individuals linked together by a set of incentives and/or sanctions

for the purpose of attaining and maintaining political leadership.
Factions operate in the prefectural and the Diet legislative bodies. [3]
Because of cross-national uncertainty over the meaning of party
identification, we shall focus on one major component of it, the
chief organizational determinant in the assemblymen's election.
We note that faction may be the dominant organizational base for
legislators and koenkai, the individual support organization for each
legislator. Koenkai perhaps translates most succinctly as personal
support organization, but it has a broader meaning. Although both
factions and koenkai are examples of vertical relationships (leader-
follower arrangements) so common in Japanese society, koenkai
organizations are much larger in size, and they are different in
purpose. The individual for whom the koenkai is organized gains
the services of his followers on the basis of particularistic criteria.
Place, family ties, and a web of reciprocal loyalties and obligations,
often developed over generations, unite seemingly disparate followers behind the individual political candidate in a manner remi-
niscent of the villagers' relationship to their village leaders in
Tokugawa Japan. [4]

Kanagawa and Shimane prefectures, our units of analysis,
present polar contrasts. Kanagawa prefecture reflects ecologically
that part of Japan which is industrial, "modern," and "developed." [5]
By comparison, Shimane represents rural, agricultural, and hence
"underdeveloped" Japan. If electoral support mechanisms differ at
different levels of socioeconomic development, this should be reflected in a comparative analysis of the two prefectures. Kanagawa
is among the most urban (91.7 percent) and most populous of all the
prefectures. In 1970, its population was 5,472,247 (third of the 46
prefectures) in contrast to Tottori, which had the lowest population
of all the prefectures, 568,777, and Tokyo, with a population of
11,408,701, which had the highest population. Shimane is forty-
third out of the 46 prefectures, with a 1970 population of 773,575.
The contrasts between the two prefectures become more significant
if standard indices of industrialization are considered. Throughout
Japan, in 1970, the census divided the labor force into 19.4 percent
primary, 33.9 percent secondary, and 46.7 percent tertiary industries.

In Kanagawa (1970), the level of industrial activity was much
higher. Only 4 percent of the labor force was engaged in primary
industrial activity, whereas 44.9 percent and 51.5 percent were
employed in secondary and tertiary industries, respectively. In
Shimane, by contrast, 38.8 percent of the labor force were employed
in primary industries, and there were 21.1 percent in secondary
and 40.1 percent in tertiary industries. While the average per
capita income in Japan was 520,250 yen in 1970, Kanagawa residents

enjoyed a considerably higher per capita income level of 623,821 yen. Per capita income in Shimane was well below the national average, at 384,971 yen. Finally, migration, both immigration and emigration, suggests the direction social and economic changes are taking. Again, the prefectures differ. From October 1, 1969, to September 30, 1970, Kanagawa showed a large net immigration of 123,125. During the same period, Shimane showed a net emigration of 11,975.

If the socioeconomic environment that is presumably supportive[6] of a high level of political party institutionalization exists anywhere in Japan, it seems reasonable to expect to find it in Kanagawa. If the political parties have been successful anywhere in Japan at the prefectural level, in terms of generating loyalty, support, and control, we assume this may be seen in Kanagawa, where local interest groups of all types have been under pressure to adapt to a rapidly changing socioeconomic environment.

Relative to most prefectures (and clearly Kanagawa), Shimane presents a socioeconomic climate that is rural and agriculturally oriented. If organizational models such as koenkai are still strong anywhere in Japan, they are likely to be so in Shimane.

Data for the Kanagawa Prefectural Assembly were collected in 1969-70 from incumbents elected in 1967 (see Appendix C for questions and code used). In that election, which generated the lowest turnout rate in the postwar period (61.9 percent), the LDP received 39.22 percent of the votes; the Socialist Party, 26.38 percent; the Democratic Socialist Party, 10.31 percent; Komei Party, 7.79 percent; the Japan Communist Party, 4.55 percent; and Independents, 11.75 percent. Primary data are drawn from 71 assemblymen responding to our interviews and questionnaires out of the 91 possible respondents, which equals 77.2 percent of all the legislators. The distribution of party strength is shown in Table 5.1.

Data from the Shimane Prefectural assemblymen were collected in 1972. In Shimane, 98 percent of the assemblymen responded to our request for interviews and questionnaires. Only one LDP member was not available. The LDP dominated the Shimane Prefectural Assembly, holding 66.9 percent of the seats. While the Japan Socialist Party is in second place, it captured only 11.9 percent of the seats, a much lower percentage than in Kanagawa. The remaining parties have either only one seat or, in the case of the Komei Party, are not represented (see Table 5.2 for the composition of the Shimane Prefectural Assembly).

TABLE 5.1

Composition of the Kanagawa Assembly,
by Parliamentary Groups

Groups	Number of Assemblymen	Percentage of Seats
Liberal Democratic Party	41	44.56
Japan Socialist Party	26	28.26
Komei Party	9	9.79
Democratic Socialist Party	8	8.69
Japan Communist Party	2	2.18
Independents	6	6.52
Total	92*	100.00

*The legal membership of the Assembly is 95. At the time
this research was conducted (1969-70), three assemblymen had
died, leaving 92 members.

Source: Compiled by the authors.

TABLE 5.2

Composition of the Shimane Assembly,
by Parliamentary Groups

Groups	Number of Assemblymen	Percentage of Seats
Liberal Democratic Party	29	66.90
Japan Socialist Party	5	11.90
Democratic Socialist Party	1	2.38
Japan Communist Party	1	2.38
Independents	6	14.28
Total	42	100.00

Source: Compiled by the authors.

THE ANALYSIS

Although theoretically possible, it is unlikely that party organization at the local community level will be well articulated if it is lacking at the prefectural levels. The same is true of the other possible electoral support mechanisms. Our major dependent variable is constructed out of the question that asked the assemblymen to rank the importance of koenkai, faction, and party for their election, that is, "Which was the chief determinant in your election?"

Table 5.3 summarizes the relationships found between our dependent variable, which ranks the importance of koenkai, faction, and political party, with independent variables that potentially have a bearing on it. The table presents Cramer Vs computed with the respondents from Shimane and Kanagawa combined and separated. We use Cramer's V coefficient of association, a nonparametric measure, to assess the relative importance of each variable.* In keeping with our original research goal, Table 5.3 allows us to answer two questions: (1) Which factors are most highly related to electoral support?, and (2) What differences and similarities exist between our two prefectures?

Examination of the Cramer Vs documents the relative <u>stability</u> of electoral support patterns in both Shimane and Kanagawa. Age and the number of candidates from the same political party are more significant in Shimane than in Kanagawa. However, the variations are minor or can be accounted for.† In fact, the independent

---

*Cramer's V is defined as follows:

$$V = \sqrt{\frac{1}{N \, Min \, (r-1, \, c-1)}}$$

where Min (r-1, c-1) refers to the minimum of the two values: (r-1) or (c-1). This coefficient is particularly useful because it corrects for the condition of the phi coefficient having no upper limit beyond the two-by-two case and varies between 0.0 and 1.0 for all tables, regardless of the number of rows and columns. Hence, a coefficient of .30 may be considered a strong association. For the two-by-two case, Cramer's V is identical to the phi measure.

†Political party organization is significant for the opposition parties, and their small numbers in Shimane accounts for the significance of this variable. As indicated in Tables 4.1 and 4.2, the LDP is more dominant in Shimane, and the LDP is the party largely affected by the problem of intraparty competition by candidates in the election.

variables do not vary significantly across the two prefectures: in these two prefectures, which differ greatly in terms of their levels of socioeconomic development, the factors associated with electoral support are virtually the same. We thus feel justified in merging the data from the two prefectures for the remaining examination of those variables found to be statistically significant. If we accept .25 as our statistical cutoff point, this allows us to eliminate three variables, public office experience, number of times elected, and attainment of the House speakership, from further analysis.

TABLE 5.3

Dependent Variable: Relative Importance of Party, Faction, Koenkai, and Independent Variables (Cramer's V): Kanagawa and Shimane

Independent Variables	Kanagawa and Shimane	Kanagawa	Shimane
Political party identification	.34	.42	.40
Age	.44	.24	.44
Number of times elected	.18	.17	.24
Father's occupation	.39	.50	.44
Occupation	.33	.36	.37
Organizational executive post	.28	.37	.35
Relative's public office experience	.72	.71	.73
Public office experience	.21	.28	.32
Political party experience	.42	.50	.38
House speakership	.08	.09	.18
Number of candidates per district from same party	.27	.25	.44
Political ambition	.46	.50	.57
Importance of present post for attainment of other public offices in future	.40	.35	.54

Source: Compiled by the authors.

We reemphasize that these generalizations apply to our two prefectures only and at one point in time. Other possibilities remain to account for the relative similarity between the two prefectures. Although Kanagawa and Shimane are at high and low poles of socioeconomic development in Japan, the range between them may not be sufficient to show variation. Alternatively, prefectures are not closed systems isolated from other prefectures and the central government, and the similarities found in Shimane and Kanagawa may indeed exist in other prefectures. When we control for political party identification—for example, the absence or low number of party members in Shimane—most of the differences that do emerge between the two prefectures "wash out." Overall, however, it is interesting to note that only 10 percent of the Shimane assemblymen, as compared with 46 percent of their Kanagawa counterparts, identified political party as their chief referent group in electoral support activities. In addition, none of the LDP assemblymen in Shimane named party as their chief electoral support mechanism, whereas in Kanagawa, 19.5 percent of the Liberal Democrats chose party.

Let us then turn to the remaining variables and examine in detail the relative importance of koenkai, factions, and parties. When we subtract the 21 nonrespondents from Kanagawa and the one nonrespondent from Shimane, we are left with 112 respondents. Because of the fairly small number of respondents, we shall rely on the combined impact of the variables rather than introduce controls, which would result in cells with too few entries.

We begin with Table 5.4, which relates political party identification to our index. Koenkai ranks first, with over one-half (59.82 percent) of the respondents. The dominance of koenkai is clear if koenkai-party and/or factions are added. Political party does rate first with 36 respondents, largely from the opposition parties. Perhaps surprisingly, faction is considered most important by only two respondents, both of them from Shimane. Of course, in Shimane, the members of the House of Representatives are elected at large in the prefecture. Hence, factions there may have a greater opportunity to penetrate to the prefectural level. Kanagawa, by comparison, has three districts, and competition between the factions may be less acute.

When we compare political party identification to our measure of electoral organizational support, the LDP contributes most heavily (50) to the dominance of koenkai. Although we separate them here, most observers would add the independents, all of whom chose koenkai, to the Liberal Democratic column. Many see the LDP as the repository of tradition and hence "less modern" than the other parties. If LDP strength continues to erode, there will yet be a

TABLE 5.4

Political Party Identification and Ranked Importance of
Koenkai, Political Party, and Faction

Party	Koenkai	Faction	Party	Koenkai-Party and/or Faction Balanced	Total Number
Liberal Democratic Party					
Percent	75.75	3.0	10.60	10.60	
Number	50	2	7	7	66
Japan Socialist Party					
Percent	16.66	0.00	83.33	0.00	
Number	4	0	20	—	24
Democratic Socialist Party					
Percent	50.00	0.00	50.00	0.00	
Number	3	0	3	—	6
Komei Party					
Number	0	0	4	0	4
Japan Communist Party					
Number	1	0	2	0	3
Independents					
Number	9	0	0	0	9
Total					
Number	67	2	36	7	112
Percent	59.82	1.78	32.14	6.24	100.00

Source: Compiled by the authors.

movement toward reliance on political party organization. We will present ideas on this conjecture below.

Turning to age as an explanatory variable, we examine the hypothesis that the greater the trend toward political party electoral support, the greater the tendency for younger representatives to rely on party versus koenkai for support in elections. This hypothesis is based on the argument that "new" political socialization patterns are most likely to have an impact on younger politicians.[7] Table 5.5 does not support this hypothesis. If we designate the 55-and-under group younger (for Japanese politicians, this is considered young) and the 56-and-over group older, it is correct that 38 out of 67 assemblymen, slightly more than one-half, are in the 56-and-over group and fall into the koenkai support column as well. Among the group of assemblymen who chose political party as their primary preference, 19 out of 36 fall into the 55-and-under group. However, two of the youngest assemblymen (45 and under) preferred faction. The results do not indicate a movement in the direction of party or koenkai.

Tables 5.6 and 5.7 compare father's occupation (a central social background variable of the assemblymen) and their own occupation to our electoral organizational support index. Overall, it is interesting to note the predominance of the self-employed group (72 out of 104 who responded to the question) in the father's occupation table. Looking at the occupation of the assemblymen themselves, we note a shift away from the self-employed category toward the public-officials-related column. However, even with this shift to more professional and public-related careers, the pattern of support preference is quite similar in both tables.

To shift to the kind of experience related to the assemblymen themselves, we asked the respondents to indicate their own backgrounds in terms of organizational posts. The working hypothesis here is that the greater the tendency for support to come from national organizations, the lower the level of dependency on local organizations, such as koenkai. Table 5.8 tests this hypothesis by relating the measure of assemblymen's previous organizational post experience to the koenkai, faction, and party index. At first, it appears that here we have clear evidence that organizational experience in labor unions, which are to be considered national organizations, produce a reliance on party support. However, if we focus on the Japan Socialist Party members,* we find that they

---

*An overwhelming majority (81.4 percent) of the people who chose political party who held labor-related organization executive posts are Socialists.

TABLE 5.5

Age and Ranked Importance of Koenkai, Party, and Faction

Age	Koenkai		Faction		Party		Koenkai–Party and/or Faction Balanced		Total Number
	Number	Percent	Number	Percent	Number	Percent	Number	Percent	
45 and below	10	56.63	2	10.52	6	31.57	1	5.26	19
46–55	19	54.28	0	0.00	13	37.14	3	8.57	35
56–65	24	60.00	0	0.00	13	32.50	3	7.50	40
Over 65	14	77.77	0	0.00	4	22.22	0	0.00	18
Total number	67		2		36		7		112

Source: Compiled by the authors.

TABLE 5.6

Father's Occupation and Ranked Importance of Koenkai, Party, and Faction

Father's Occupation	Koenkai		Faction		Party		Koenkai–Party and/or Faction Balanced		Total Number
	Number	Percent	Number	Percent	Number	Percent	Number	Percent	
Self-employed (small- to medium-sized businessmen, fishermen, farmers)	46	63.88	1	1.38	20	27.77	5	6.93	72
Blue-collar workers	1	50.00	0	0.00	1	50.00	0	0.00	2
White-collar workers	2	50.00	0	0.00	2	50.00	0	0.00	4
Public officials	9	69.23	1	7.69	2	15.38	1	7.69	13
Others	6	46.16	0	0.00	7	53.84	0	0.00	13
Subtotal number	64		2		32		6		104*
Number not available	3	37.50	0	0.00	4	50.00	1	12.50	8
Total	67		2		36		7		112

*Actual responses to question.
Source: Compiled by the authors.

TABLE 5.7

Occupation and Ranked Importance of Koenkai, Party, and Faction

Occupation	Koenkai		Faction		Party		Koenkai-Party and/or Faction Balanced		Total Number
	Number	Percent	Number	Percent	Number	Percent	Number	Percent	
Self-employed (small- to medium sized businessmen, farmers, fishermen)	41	71.92	0	0.00	10	17.54	6	10.52	57
Blue-collar workers	2	14.28	0	0.00	12	85.71	0	0.00	14
White-collar workers	4	80.00	0	0.00	1	20.00	0	0.00	5
Public officials, secretaries of Diet members, professionals	14	58.33	2	8.33	8	33.33	0	0.00	24
Other organizations	6	50.00	0	0.00	5	41.66	1	8.33	12
Total number	67		2		36		7		112

Source: Compiled by the authors.

TABLE 5.8

Organizational Executive Post and Ranked Importance of Koenkai, Party, and Faction

Organizational Executive Post	Koenkai		Faction		Party		Koenkai–Party and/or Faction Balanced		Total Number
	Number	Percent	Number	Percent	Number	Percent	Number	Percent	
Labor-related organizations	7	25.91	—	—	20	74.09	—	—	27
Farm-related organizations	19	76.00	—	—	3	12.00	3	12.00	25
Business and professional organizations	12	75.00	—	—	3	18.75	1	6.25	16
Local organizations	12	75.00	—	—	2	12.50	2	12.50	16
Others	9	65.71	1	7.41	3	21.42	1	7.41	14
Subtotal number	59		1		31		7		98*
Number not available	8		1		5		0		14
Total number	67		2		36		7		112*

*Actual responses to question.
Source: Compiled by the authors.

constitute the group which relies heavily on labor organizations for support, that is, an overwhelming majority of ex-labor-related organization executives who identified the party as the most important factor in their electoral success were Socialists. This evidence, then, supports the view that labor unions are the Japan Socialist Party's substitute for koenkai.[8]

On the other hand, a great number of koenkai-oriented assemblymen are related to the local-based organizations. For the legislators who have had farm coop and other farmer-related organizational experiences in executive posts, 76.0 percent ranked koenkai higher than faction or party support. Likewise, 75.0 percent of local organization executives, such as local fire squad captains, youth group leaders, and town association officials, preferred koenkai over faction or party. It is interesting to note that Japanese farmer organizations are typically villagewide affairs.[9] Thus, both local organizations and farm coops constitute local bases for electoral and other political activities. A large proportion of assemblymen who see koenkai as being of primary significance have local organization bases.

Finally, out of the ambition-related questions, Table 5.9 presents the data on those who prefer koenkai as opposed to faction or party, providing more evidence (along with the variable age, see Table 5.5) for understanding the current direction, either toward or away from koenkai as the major basis of electoral support.[10] Those who answered no to the question, "Do you consider the present post as the last public office?" are considered ambitious for higher political posts. Out of the group that listed koenkai as their major support vehicle, 38 out of 65 assemblymen (60 percent) who responded answered no or indicated latent ambition. In comparison, 16 out of the 30 respondents who listed party as their chief electoral support mechanism indicated ambition. If there were a movement from koenkai toward party—we have noted no movement— perhaps, there is a positive relationship between ambitious political figures and political party.

CONCLUSION

What does the analysis indicate? Surprisingly, party is the only major contending force with koenkai. We offer the following comments. Table 5.4 indicates that the opposition parties uniformly nominated political party as more important than koenkai. Yet when we analyzed the relationships between koenkai versus party and the selected independent variables, we found that the differences were not especially significant (with the exception of Table 5.8,

TABLE 5.9

Political Ambition and Ranked Importance of Koenkai, Party, and Faction

Political Ambition	Koenkai		Faction		Party		Koenkai-Party and/or Faction Balanced		Total
	Number	Percent	Number	Percent	Number	Percent	Number	Percent	Number
Yes (no ambition)	27	60.00	0	0.00	16	35.55	2	4.44	45
No (political ambition)	26	66.66	2	5.13	7	17.94	4	10.25	39
Other (latent political ambition)	12	60.00	0	0.00	7	35.00	1	5.00	20
Japan Communist Party cases	0	0.00	0	0.00	2	100.00	0	0.00	2
Subtotal	65		2		32		7		106
Not available	2	33.33	0	0.00	4	66.66	0	0.00	6
Total number	67		2		36		7		112

Source: Compiled by the authors.

which deals with the relationship between organizational executive posts and our ranked index of koenkai, faction, and party preference). The answer, as others have hinted, may rest in the term political party. To a large extent, unions for the Japan Socialist Party, "cells" for the Communist Party, and Sokagakkai for the Komei Party may be considered as substitutes for party organization and, for that matter, koenkai itself. It follows that the relationships are often not as significant as one might forecast. But we must not ignore the significant differences that are indicated by the data. The LDP and their allied independents rely on koenkai much more than the opposition parties, and this holds up throughout the relationships and across the two compared prefectural assemblies. The LDP appears to be secure as the dominant party in both Kanagawa and Shimane for at least the immediate future, and so a continued major role for koenkai may be projected as well.

Theoretically, the data suggest that there is relatively little organizational connection between the assemblymen and their national political party counterparts. This, in turn, suggests other inferences. One of the central functions of political parties is to act as the intervening variable between the public and the government,[11] transmission belts indicating issue preferences on the part of the public. In both Shimane and Kanagawa, we found that party and even faction are not significant support factors for the assemblymen. Therefore, it is difficult to see how the Japanese political party system, per se, can operate as its proponents indicate it does. This is not to suggest that the parties do not respond to the public or that they are not important. The political parties, especially the LDP, may remain national and Diet-centered.[12] Since, in Shimane and Kanagawa, the assemblymen do not respond, behave, or think in terms of party, it is easier for political reference poles to continue to be built around organizational models like koenkai. We may suggest that there is little incentive for local community organizations to develop strong ties to the national political parties when parties are not salient at the prefectural level.

Political parties may indeed be important, along with factions, at the national level. But they are not salient at the prefectural level and, by inference, not important at the local level either.*

---

*There is another interesting point that John Kringen suggested to us. Reacting to work done on Japanese parties, we may have inadvertently implied an image of highly institutionalized party systems at the local level (Western Europe and U.S. model). Comparative work on this question needs to be done.

Rather, we wish to argue that we should view <u>koenkai itself as the institutionalized medium of electoral support at the prefectural level</u>. In both Shimane and Kanagawa, at very different levels of socioeconomic development, koenkai is the crucial support mechanism—and this in a country that began to develop a political party system in the 1880s, at roughly the same time, or in some cases before, party systems developed in Europe. At least in the prefectures studied, the organizational progression in elite-mass organizational support expected from the political development literature was not found. Thus, it seems reasonable to us to suggest that in the case of koenkai, here is yet another instance where a model elaborated from the existing organizational models has proven entirely adaptable in a society now entering the postindustrial era, a set of findings congruent with the collective goods approach. Is there really any logical reason to suggest that this will not continue to be the case?

NOTES

1. Perhaps the best statement of this position with respect to Japan remains the several chapters on interest groups, political parties, local government, and so forth. in Robert E. Ward, ed., <u>Political Development in Modern Japan</u> (Princeton, N.J.: Princeton University Press, 1965). The assumption that socioeconomic change necessarily causes common political, social and cultural convergences in societies that have industrialized has been criticized. See Bernard Karsh and Robert E. Cole, "Industrialization and the Convergence Hypothesis: Some Aspects of Contemporary Japan," <u>Journal of Social Issues</u> 24 (October 1968): 45-64. Compare Ian Weinberg, "The Problem of the Convergence of Industrial Societies: A Critical Look at the State of a Theory," <u>Comparative Studies in Society and History</u> 11 (January 1969): 1-15.

2. James W. White, "Tradition and Politics in Studies of Contemporary Japan," <u>World Politics</u> 26 (April 1974): 400-27. Compare Joseph R. Gusfield, "Tradition and Modernity: Misplaced Polarities in the Study of Social Change," <u>American Journal of Sociology</u> 72 (January 1967): 351-62.

3. For a recent review of the literature, see Haruhiro Fukui, "Japan: In a Dominant Party System, the Case of Japan," in Frank P. Belloni and Dennis C. Beller, eds., <u>Factions and Parties</u> (Santa Barbara, Calif.: ABC-Clio Press, 1978).

4. The best discussion of koenkai is in Gerald L. Curtis, <u>Election Campaigning Japanese Style</u> (New York: Columbia University Press, 1971). Compare B. Thayer, <u>How the Conservatives</u>

Rule Japan (Princeton, N.J.: Princeton University Press, 1969), especially chap. 4.

5. Data sources for the ecological description include Kanagawa-ken, ed., Kensei Digest (1969) and Kanagawa-ken, kikaku chōsabu tokeichōsaka (Statistics Survey Section, Planning and Research Department, Kanagawa Prefecture), ed., Kensei yōran [Prefectural Census Survey] (Yokohama: Kanagawa-ken, 1969); for Kanagawa and Shimane prefectures, Kanagawa-ken, kikaku chōsabu tokeichōsaka (Statistics Survey Section, Planning and Research Department, Kanagawa Prefecture), ed., Kensei yōran [Prefectural Census Survey] (Yokohama: Kanagawa-ken, 1972), and Shimane-ken (Shimane Prefecture), Kensei yōran [Prefectural Census Survey] (1972); for Shimane as well, Sōrifu tōkeikyoku (Bureau of Statistics, Office of the Prime Minister), Jyuminfotoku jinkoido hokoku nenpo (1967-72).

6. Chong Lim Kim, "Socio-Economic Development and Political Democracy in Japanese Prefectures," American Political Science Review 65 (March 1971): 184-86.

7. For a discussion of the importance of age as an explanatory variable, see Kenneth Prewitt, The Recruitment of Political Leaders: A Study of Citizen-Politicians (Indianapolis, Ind.: Bobbs-Merrill, 1970).

8. See Masao Soma, Nihon no senkyo [Japanese elections] (Tokyo: Ushio Shuppansha, 1967), p. 96. For a standard textbook statement on this substitute role, see Hajime Shinohara and Yonosuke Nagai, eds., "Seiji katei ni okeru shudanka" [The trend toward groups formation in the political process] in Gendai seijigaku nyumon [An introduction to contemporary political science] (Tokyo: Yuhikaku, 1965).

9. Takeshi Ishida, Gendai soshiki-ron [Contemporary organization theory] (Tokyo: Iwanami Shoten, 1961).

10. On the importance of ambition in politics, see Joseph A. Schlesinger, Ambition and Politics (Chicago: Rand McNally, 1966), and, more recently, Kenneth Prewitt, "Political Ambitions, Volunteerism, and Electoral Accountability," American Political Science Review 64 (March 1970): 5-17. Compare Kan Ori, "Amerikagashukoku ni okeru gunkenjishoku no seijiteki seikaku ni kansuru ichi kōsatsu" [American political and prosectorial office] Amerika Kenkyu 7 (1973): 145-68.

11. See David E. Apter, The Politics of Modernization (Chicago: University of Chicago Press, 1965), 181-82.

12. For the larger comparative view on political party institutionalization, see Kenneth Janda, A Conceptual Framework for the Comparative Analysis of Political Parties, Comparative Politics Series, vol. 1 (Beverly Hills, Calif.: Sage Publications, 1970).

6
POLITICAL ECONOMY AND POSTINDUSTRIALIZATION IN JAPANESE POLITICS

In this study, we have described the evolution of the political party system in Japan and attempted to show, through statistical analysis, that it is reasonably stable and enduring. In order to account for the particular nature of change and stability, we examined the interface between endogenous models, such as habatsu (factions), koenkai (personal support organizations), and the party system itself.

How shall we relate this analysis of the political party system to basic patterns in Japanese society and politics? If Japan is a postindustrial society, does Japan remain a stable polity with an economic and social system that will continue to avoid the conflict and stress so evident in other postindustrial states? Or are conflict and change on the horizon? Certainly, a number of recent studies by distinguished students of Japanese politics are not oblivious to signs of change, as symbolized by the decade-old Narita Airport controversy, the growth of political power at the local level, and the greater uncertainty of whether economic growth should be pursued at the cost of all other goals.[1]

In fact, most of these and other major works on Japanese politics may be placed under the pluralist vision of politics, modified, perhaps, to include the corporate framework that would seem to fit Japanese politics so well. For our part, while recognizing the importance of these efforts, we are persuaded that Japan is on the brink of substantial socioeconomic and political transformation, a set of changes that puts a new set of boundaries within which we should place the party system itself. We end this book with (1) data to answer the questions: Is Japan a postindustrial society? and, Do the projections made about the political economy make sense?;

(2) an argument for new limits for Japanese politics, suggested by the theory traditions from political economy; and (3) some projections concerning the role of the party system itself.

POSTINDUSTRIALIZATION AND THE JAPANESE CASE

Whether one accepts or rejects the views of the pluralists about Japan or the unreconstructed critiques of orthodox Marxists depends squarely on the images and assumptions one holds about the nature and direction of Japanese political change itself. There is a new vision of politics now emerging that uses one or another of two sets of theory traditions from political economy to develop a very different view of the present state of the Japanese political process and prospects for the future. This vision sees merit in projections that suggest the Japanese are really just entering the age of politics, that we may indeed expect a continued rise in political participation and decline of authority structures at central governmental levels, greater emphasis on equality versus liberty, and a related rise in political conflict. The first question, however, is whether Japan is a postindustrial society; we begin with a sketch of the concept post-industrialization we introduced in Chapter 1.[2]

It is always difficult to decide whether it is appropriate to use a new bench mark or continuum in thinking about sociopolitical change. Poles or bench marks such as tradition and modernity or industrial and now postindustrial society can constrain and mask as much as they highlight. It is sensible to use such labels—though always in a provisional sense—to mark apparent threshold changes in the society, economy, and polity, changes that render much of the institutional arrangements previously developed outmoded. Especially in the case of Japan, where the pace of change has been so swift, it must be recognized that new "phases" or stages are really added onto existing industrial and agricultural economic structures; the socioeconomic and political phases of change become interwoven. In any event, there is growing consensus that it indeed is not "business as usual," that socioeconomic and political change beyond the stages identified as modernization and industrialization is occurring. Intense debates about the direction and meaning of this change mark each of the social sciences concerned with macro, historical change, and it is now possible to draw the threads together into at least one mosaic that captures some of the emergent changes. In the economic system, there is a point that we might call mature industrialization, which is defined as the juncture in economic growth where manufacturing or industrial-related activities account for the greatest proportion of the gross national product. The other major areas of economic activity are usually divided into agricultural (or primary) and service (tertiary) categories. However, in a number of countries in Western Europe, North America, and, we shall argue, in Japan, industry is no longer the main engine of the economy; rather, the service sector, which especially includes governmental institutions, becomes increasingly dominant. Much of economic activity in the public sector is not, as we know, either easily measurable in terms of its efficiency nor actually capable of self-generating growth, as is the case with, for example, manufacturing goods.

Among the many implications of this changeover are three that are particularly important here. First, if many of a nation's economic activities are not encompassed by neoclassical economic criteria, we need new measures of efficiency. The alternative appears to be collective action; Japanese citizens in the largest and most powerful unions will simply raid the public treasury. Second, there may well be upper limits to the public sector, in parts or in its entirety, because of both a declining tax base provided by industry and the rise in inflation. Finally, inflation does appear to play an increasing role in the economies of the societies alluded to; perhaps this is due to the first points noted.

These societies do appear to be entering an era where both inflation and unemployment require the label post-Keynesian to be applied. It is not just rising energy costs that fuel inflation; the U.S. and British economies look increasingly like what economists call a common pool problem, a "tragedy of the commons," where in the absence of market criteria, which held down wages and costs in the industrial era, there are precious few incentives for unions to hold down their demands. Neoclassical economics was generated to describe and model capitalism, an economic phase associated with industrialization. Perhaps we now need to focus on what economists call nonmarket decision-making models. The question here is whether Japan will avoid the fate of the other postindustrial societies or share a common fate with respect to inflation and related problems.

The economic changes noted have parallels in society at large, its institutions, and the values of its citizens. Population and urbanization rise dramatically during the industrialization phase (in Japan, this begins with the Meiji Restoration) and reach their peak at the mature industrialization phase; thereafter, population growth declines to apparently a zero growth point, and the cities actually empty, as citizens move to the suburbs. Formal educational levels reach unprecedented heights, and perhaps, in addition, because of the fact that many citizens have achieved an adequate material standard of living, the focus of public policy discussion changes from an emphasis on the level, the quantity, of goods produced, to the quality of goods and services produced.[3] This indeed may be a natural evolution; in the nineteenth and twentieth centuries, citizens worked to simply establish basic social institutions on a society-wide basis. For example, educational and institutions to deliver minimum social services were founded after the onset of the Meiji Restoration. Once established, however, attention turned to the quality of education being delivered. As groups develop a better material base and more leisure time, they naturally become more critical and demanding of services to be tailored to their particular, specialized needs. More controversial research findings indicate that substantial value change at the individual level is also transforming the belief systems of publics in postindustrial societies in Europe and perhaps in Japan as well.[4] For many citizens, there is a change in emphasis from bourgeois, material wants, such as freedom and liberty and order and economic security, to self-actualization values and equality and social-psychological concerns. The increased emphasis on equality translates into demands for greater participation in decision making. Again, we would add only that there may be a natural evolution connected to this value change similar to the transformation of education concerns noted. Finally, in both discussions of economic and social change, there is substantial agreement that interdependence of all sorts increases in postindustrial societies and that information becomes a defining characteristic of the age.

REPRESENTATIVE MACRO SOCIOECONOMIC MEASURES

Let us, then, examine appropriate measures of our model to see whether and to what extent Japan is moving into the postindustrial process-state. For comparative (across time) purposes, we shall trace socioeconomic change in selected variables from the late nineteenth and early twentieth century to the mid-1970s.

Our first two graphs (see Figures 6.1 and 6.2) examine (1) the relative proportion of the economy accounted for by the primary and secondary industries and government from 1880 to 1930, and (2) the changes in relative employment in primary, secondary, and tertiary industries from 1880 to 1940. Figure 6.1 is surprising in that governmental expenditure remains relatively high in comparison with the primary and secondary industries, only beginning to decline in the late 1920s. Over the period covered, we see the rise of the industrial (secondary) sector. The primary sector declines in the late 1920s, but this is in large part due to the economic depression that struck Japan. Figure 6.2 more vividly illustrates the Japanese economy's development as an industrial power. In fact, employment in agriculture declines substantially from its peak in 1900. In comparison, the secondary and tertiary sectors begin their rapid increase

FIGURE 6.1

Expenditures: Primary, Secondary Industries, and
Government from 1880 through 1930

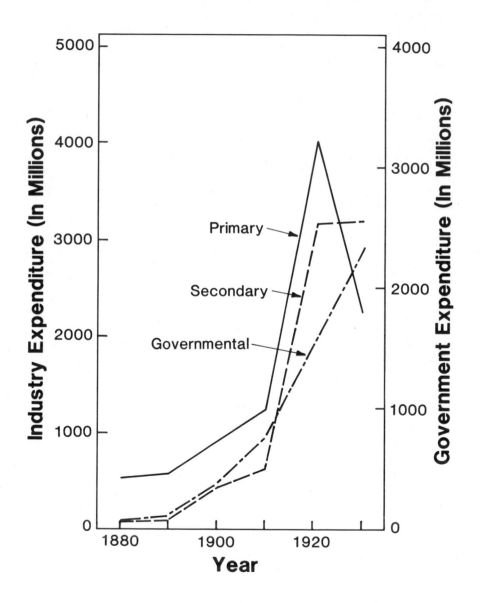

Source: Koichi Emi, Government Fiscal Activity and Economic
Growth in Japan, 1868-1960 (Tokyo: Kinokuniya Bookstore, 1968),
pp. 168-72.

FIGURE 6.2

Employment in Primary, Secondary, and Tertiary
Industries from 1880 through 1940

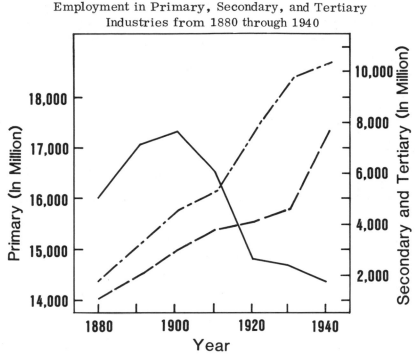

Source: Kazushi Ohkawa, The Growth Rate of the Japanese
Economy Since 1878 (Tokyo: Konokuniya Bookstore, 1957), pp.
145-245.

from 1880 onward. By contrast, we present Figure 6.3, which looks
at changes in employment patterns in agriculture, manufacturing,
service, and government from 1960 to 1977. Here, we see a pattern
that closely resembles the postindustrial process-state. Employment in agriculture continues to decline, but apparently (a five-year
time span is not conclusive), the manufacturing sector reaches its
peak in 1970, while the service and governmental sectors continue to
rise at substantial rates. Collectively these graphs indicate the
dramatic economic change in less than 100 years from a rural
agrarian-based economy to an economy that, like its European and
American counterparts, is becoming service sector oriented, that
is, oriented toward research and development activities, which contribute to a higher quality of life.

FIGURE 6.3

Employed Persons 15 Years Old and Over in Agriculture,
Manufacturing, Services, and Government from 1960 to 1977

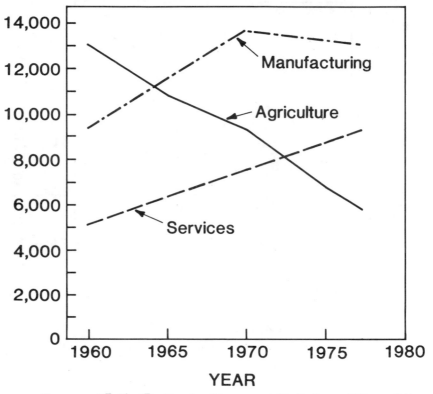

YEAR

Source: Sōrifu tōkeikyoku (Bureau of Statistics, Office of the
Prime Minister), Nihon tōkei nenkan [Japan statistical yearbook]
(Tokyo: Government Printing Office, 1978).

Next, we turn to a summary index, Figure 6.4, which we suggest captures much of the population and urbanization increase in
Japan during the past 100 years. Population per square kilometer
captures the degree of density (urbanization) and, in terms of its
rate of increase, the rise in both population pressure and urbanization. In absolute terms, population per square kilometer rises from
91.2 in 1872 to 300.5 in 1975; this indicates the dramatic change
from a rural to an urban society. However, when we examine the
rate of change in population density per square kilometer over the
100-year period, additional interpretations are appropriate. If we

FIGURE 6.4

Urbanization in Japan, 1875-1980

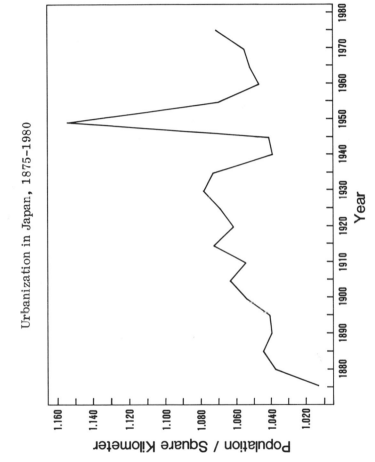

Source: Sōrifu tōkeikyoku (Bureau of Statistics, Office of the Prime Minister), Nihon tōkei nenkan [Japan statistical yearbook] (Tokyo: Government Printing Office, 1977).

draw an imaginary best least squares fit through the rate change curve, the slope would rise very quickly throughout the pre-World War II period and then begin to level off—especially if we were to factor out the rapid increase in density (urbanization) that occurred during the postwar recovery years. Actually, if we were to look only at population growth (not shown here), we would see the Japanese success in stabilizing their population after the war.

What we have seen so far is representative evidence that there has been a substantial change in the nature of the Japanese economic and social pattern of living, as measured by urbanization; it appears that Japan is moving into the postindustrial process-state. However, to complete our survey, we shall present graphs that measure the changing attention given to the national infrastructure.

If we examine the increase in total railroad mileage from 1870 to 1970 (Figure 6.5), the absolute increase is from zero in 1870 to just under 28,000 miles in 1970. If, however, we look at the change in the slope of increase after World War II, the transformation is substantial. In fact, by 1960, the rail network reached its highest point; attention turned to its maintenance, improvement, and, of course, aviation and road networks. Since 1960, the amount of total rail mileage has declined. Finally, when we look at higher education (Figure 6.6), one again sees the changeover from the construction cycle—mainly during the Meiji period (before 1920), to its maintenance and improvement, especially in recent years.

CHANGE IN THE INDIVIDUAL VALUE SYSTEM

All we have meant to suggest is an alternative way of looking at basic socioeconomic change in Japan. Although these data are simple descriptive summaries in and of themselves, they do conform with our model of the change process from modernization to postindustrialization. However, has this system-level change been accompanied by value change at the individual level? We turn to a summary of the evidence.

The structuring question is whether Japanese values have moved from an emphasis on order and deference to leaders to a greater concern for individual expression, participation, and equality in relationships.[5] Table 6.1 traces the change in Japanese attitudes toward their preferred life-style. The transformation is striking; the number of Japanese who wish to live for fulfillment of self has doubled, while the proportion of Japanese citizens prepared to "sacrifice one's life in the service of society" has been reduced by one-half over the 20-year period. The proportion of citizens sampled who are willing to leave everything in the hands of leaders has also

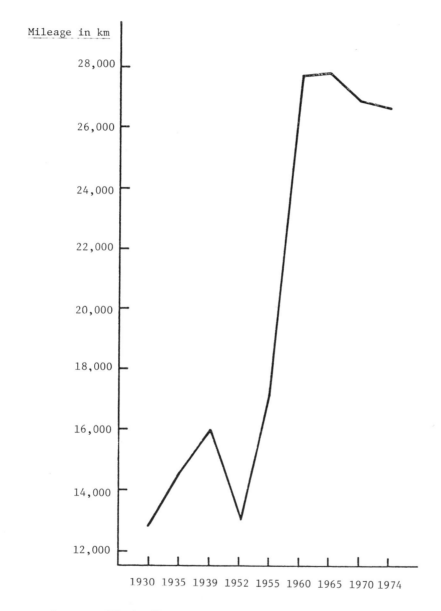

FIGURE 6.5

Railroad Mileage, 1930-74

Source: Sōrifu tōkeikyoku (Bureau of Statistics, Office of the Prime Minister), Nihon tōkei nenkan [Japan statistical yearbook] (Tokyo: Government Printing Office, 1976), pp. 254-56.

FIGURE 6.6

Education: Number of Students in Higher Education. 1890-1975

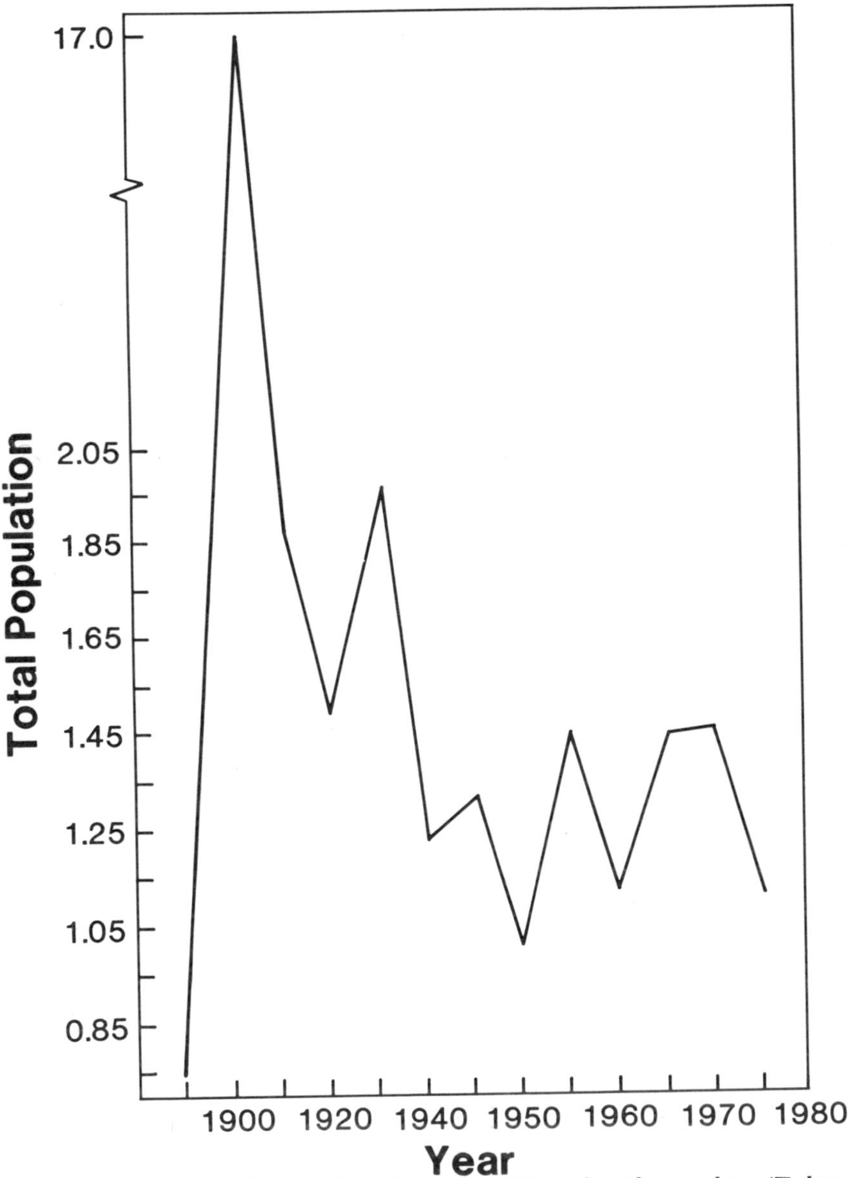

Source: Kyoikushimbunsha, ed., Nihon kyoiku nenkan (Tokyo: Kyoikushimbunsha, 1971), pp. 620-24; Kyoiku nenkan Ranko iinkai, ed., Kyoiku Nenkan (Tokyo: Gyosei, 1976, pp. 585-610; Sōrifu tokeikyoku (Bureau of Statistics, Office of the Prime Minister), ed., Nihon tōkei nenkan [Japan statistical yearbook], no. 26 (Tokyo: Government Printing Office, 1976), pp. 554-56.

TABLE 6.1

Preferred Way of Living in Japan, 1953-73
(percent)

Preferred Way of Living	1953	1958	1963	1968	1973
For self-fulfillment: to live according to one's liking without regard for money or honor	21	27	30	32	39
For comfort: to live a life of ease without worries	11	18	19	20	23
For wealth: to work hard in order to become rich	15	17	17	17	14
For integrity: to live honestly and uprightly, working against injustice in the world	29	23	18	17	11
For society: to sacrifice one's life in the service of society	10	6	6	6	5
For honor: to study hard in order to become famous	6	3	4	3	3

Source: Institute of Statistical Mathematics, Office of the Bureau of Prime Minister, National Census Reports, 1953-73 (Tokyo: Government Printing Office).

declined from 43 percent to 23 percent over the same time period; in fact; 51 percent are now opposed to this attitude. More evidence (not shown here) of the decline in unquestioning deference toward those in authority concerns the decline in party identification. The Institute of Statistical Mathematics reports 46 percent of the large 20 to 29 age group as having no party allegiance by 1973, compared to only 20 percent expressing no party identification in 1953. Overall, the segment of the public reporting no party allegiance has grown from 19 percent in 1953 to 33 percent in 1973. However, if we examine evidence concerning the type of political leader preferred, there has been virtually no change in citizen support for leadership style congruent with "traditional" organizational (personalistic, leader-follower) expectations over the 20-year period:

Suppose there are two section heads in your firm. If
you had to make a choice, under which section-head
would you prefer to work? Head A never asks you to
do unreasonable work and always sticks to the rules,
but never does any favors for you which are not directly related to the job. Head B sometimes asks you to do
extra work, even if it is against the work rules, but, on
the other hand, does favors for you even though they are
not directly related to the job. The great majority (an
average of approximately 80%) continues to prefer type
B section head. [6]

Collective Goods Theory

Thus, there is representative evidence that Japan is rapidly
becoming a postindustrial society. The problem is that without
structuring principles to order the world sketched here, one is unable to really develop coherent interpretations of the present or
make projections about the future. Writers in the pluralist tradition present confusing projections concerning the political implications of postindustrialization. There are, we feel, two sets of arguments which may be abstracted from very different theory traditions that will suggest such structuring principles. First, in Chapter 1, we introduced collective goods theory, originally developed
by neoclassical economists to handle a variety of nonmarket decision-
making problems. Second, there is critical theory, mainly developed by European critics, who are attempting to develop thorough,
radical critiques of advanced capitalist societies. The collective
goods approach centers on the individual, viewing the individual as
a being of rational choice. Collective goods adherents move from
the individual to the group, institutional, and societal level; whenever and wherever change is perceived, one looks for the mixture
of incentives and sanctions that lead individuals to change their attitudes and behavior. Critical theorists, for their part, operate at
the macro-system level and search for the society-wide patterns of
socioeconomic and political change which, they argue, create disjunctures between the state and society, the individual and institutions—disjunctures that dictate wholesale social and political change.
The extraordinary point, unacknowledged by either of these schools,
is that their arguments converge to similar points on a number of
issues, points which, we shall argue below, support our argument
that politics itself is undergoing a full-scale redefinition. The limits of politics are indeed being redrawn and extended. Here, we
shall note only the essential structure of each school.

We indicated the collective goods approach begins with the assumption of individual rational choice; when confronted with the necessity of choice, the individual is assumed to make comparative cost and benefit calculations. Now, economists do not make assumptions about either the ranking of preferences in individual utility schedules or what the content of preference schedules comprises. By modeling the environment within which the individual exists, however, one can make such assumptions. In fact, in modeling the characteristics of postindustrialization that is what we are doing. However, the heart of the collective goods approach rests on the distinctions between classes of goods, on the one hand, and economies and diseconomies of scale flowing from organizations (institutions) that deliver these goods to publics of differential size and scope, on the other hand.

Goods are whatever we want, from material things to social-psychological needs. Economists, following Samuelson, distinguish between public and private goods. Private goods are, by virtue of the nature of their production, divisible; if the producer and consumer agree on the price of a Honda, a consumable good, presumably both are satisfied. There is no confusion here about who is to pay what proportion of the costs or to whom the benefits are to accrue. Analytically, at the other pole of the continuum of goods are public goods. By dint of the joint nature of their production, goods such as national defense, law and order, and fire protection are deemed (at least in theory) to be indivisible; if produced for one member of the community, these goods may not be denied any member of that community. We noted previously that with public goods comes the free rider problem, for in the absence of the threat of sanction, individuals have only public spiritedness to lead them to pay for a public good, for example, public television, which they can consume for free. Collective goods really comprise what economists view as a large residual category between public and private goods. These are the goods with externalities attached, which, as noted in Chapter 1, inevitably result in conflict. We will return to link these distinctions to our sketch of postindustrialization in Japan, but first, we need to describe the importance of economies and diseconomies of scale.

In size rests greater efficiency of performance, both in terms of quality and costs—so assume most sociological theories of organizations and institutions. Greater size brings greater numbers of specialists, who then can develop the critical mass necessary for proper coordination and planning—hence, the greater the size of the organization, the greater the economies of scale. Indeed, the twentieth century empirically documents movement away from decentralized, social, economic, and political arrangements toward centralized institutions. Of course, the Japanese successfully developed their country economically from the top down headed by centralized institutional political arrangements. From collective goods theory, however, comes a very different set of expectations about the relationship between size and economies and diseconomies of scale. Again, let us return to the rational choice assumption. Instead of trumpeting the virtues of increased functional-specificity in large organizations, one again simply assumes that the individuals will act so as to minimize costs or maximize gains. Organizations place individuals in hierarchical relationship to one another. Whereas functional theorists argue that larger numbers of people performing carefully defined roles is virtuous, the collective goods approach looks carefully at the number of levels in an organization. Here, one dismisses the functionalist view of organizations and, from the rational choice assumption, assumes the basic goal of individuals in the organization is to simply maintain their job or improve their chances for advancement in the organization. The inferior in the bureaucratic structure will report information he or she thinks the superior wishes to hear, not what the superior should hear. Information that forces supervisors to make decisions is assumed to be unwelcome because actual decision making necessitates choice, and that is in itself risky. From collective goods theory, we are led to assume that the greater the number of vertical channels information must pass through, the greater the tendency of information distortion. Collective goods theorists are prepared to assume that diseconomies, not economies, of scale result from centralization of organizations.

Finally, we now need to connect up the points about economies and diseconomies of scale and the distinctions between goods. The fundamental point is straightforward. Surely we need to think more carefully about which goods should be delivered to which publics (themselves increasingly variegated) by which size governmental organizations. Some goods that are more nearly "pure" public in nature may indeed be delivered by large centralized public institutions. Here, we are thinking not only of national defense, but air and water pollution control or any good that is not significantly information sensitive in the sense of requiring the multiple sender-receiver interactions that result in the formation distortion alluded to, which, in turn, leads to decline in efficiency of the goods produced. Next, we must consider the point that publics (catchments in economics) must themselves be distinguished. Collective goods are typically not well served by large centralized institutions, and if our argument, presented below, that collective goods are coming to dominate the public agenda in postindustrial Japan has merit, the largely centralized institutions developed in earlier periods of

Japanese history become suspect. Why are collective goods—about which conflict is inevitable because of the points noted above—rising? There are at least four reasons. First, as socioeconomic development continues, citizens apparently become more aware of the negative externalities they are forced to consume; previously, they may have been willing to consume the effects of pollution, but in the 1970s the Kogai no mondai ("pollution problem") becomes a major public issue. It does not matter if the pollution emanates from public or private sources; it is considered a collective good. Second, citizens and public bureaucrats, in an unspoken conspiracy, demand that government itself provide more collective goods. For their part, citizens not only want the handicapped to be provided for, they want special transportation or educational provisions. Having developed the basic social services, bureaucrats—for reasons of inter- and intraorganization competition for budgets—search for new areas of application in the public sector. Third, public provision of goods previously provided for in the private sector, and thought to be private goods, tends to drive out the remaining private provision of those goods. Public provision of higher education, for example, leads to a decline in the public's willingness to support private institutions of higher learning. Four, recall that interdependence is associated with postindustrial society. There may well be many positive points about increased interdependence, but there is also a rise in the possibility of negative externalities attached to such interdependence. We shall return to the implications of this sketch of collective goods analytics for political change in Japan, but first, we shall note the main arguments of the critical theory school.

Critical Theory

Critical theorists depart from Marxist critiques of social and economic change to argue whether or not system-wide transformation is apt to take place. From Marxism itself comes the argument that capitalism is a historical epoch, part of the process of historical evolution. Arguing from the perspective of the society, critical theorists look for symptoms of the breakdown of systems of economic and political integration. Members of this school are hostile to capitalism and criticize the domination of the working class by the bourgeoisie. Like Marxists of previous eras, they see the activities of capitalism in the international system—in the being of multinational corporations—as imperialism that flourishes off Third World states, which are dependent on (in dependent status to) these corporate arrangements. More importantly, theorists such as Gramsci and Habermas alert us to the need to view our institutional

systems, our very basic conceptualizations of authority, political
leadership, the state, and so forth, as themselves mechanisms of
legitimation for particular models of control.[7] Language itself may
be seen as legitimating and reflecting the dominant authority systems of an historical epoch. Always thinking in historical terms,
critical theorists see the particular form of control or forms of
domination, for example, definitions of property, conceptualizations
of the economy, the state, and their relationships, as being tied to
specific historical periods. They recognize the productive powers
of capitalism, but feel, with postindustrial theorists, that economic
change is rendering the productive sector of the economy obsolete.
Unlike postindustrial and collective goods theorists, they do not
view the state as simply adjudicating among the various interest
groups in society contending for power or as a nuisance to be reduced. Rather, the state is viewed as an essential element of the
system of domination in society. The state may form a new "middle
strata" that seeks to maintain itself through a variety of legitimation models.

The second contribution of the critical theory school may be
encompassed under the concept of hegemony. Through understandings attached to ideology, property, and so forth, as to what actually constitutes proper authority, leadership, and decision-making
arrangements, the dominant class in society maintain their position
of power. In Gramsci's evocation of hegemony, the customs, norms,
and even values of a society underwrite the particular mosaic of
class relationship extant in any society. Language systems become
modes of domination because of tacit meanings governing relationships between words. Authority and leadership, for example, are,
in capitalist societies, understood to mean hierarchical systems of
relationships between individuals and groups who are placed in asym-
metrical arrangements with each other. In societies in other historical epochs, though, the understandings, the vocabulary describing authority and leadership, are quite different. Thus, the Gramscian
contribution is to "liberate" and broaden the cultural and political dimensions of society from their status as epiphenomena strictly determined by the economic model of production under orthodox Marxism.
Moreover, in addition to sweeping historical critiques of modern
capitalism, critical theorists look for disjunctures between particular macro-institutionalized systems of domination and the individual
classes governed by them. For example, Offe points to the emer-
gence of disjunctures between authority systems at the macro-
societal level and micro, individual, and group levels in advanced
capitalist societies. In other words, while the largely hierarchical
socioeconomic and political institutions of society remain in place,
very different types of authority arrangements are developing at the

micro level, for example, on the workshop floor itself in factories. Workers, in fact, are increasingly unwilling to put up with hierarchical authority systems and the related absence of control over their own destinies. Certainly, it is instructive to consider how the concept participation itself has been changed in meaning over the past two or three decades. In the major works in Japanese political science of the 1950s and 1960s, political participation was understood to comprise a largely reactive and passive component; it was the job of elites to govern and the role of citizens to comply, though they might object to the decisions if they desired. Political participation in Japan now includes a much more direct and active sharing of decision making.

The Political Consequences of Postindustrialization

Now, let us bring these two schools to bear on the question of the political consequences of postindustrialization in Japan; in both schools, we find arguments, often converging, to support the redefinition of the limits of politics thesis.

From the perspectives of collective goods theory and critical theory, the import of the crisis of the state diagnosed by commentators becomes clearer on several counts, and we are led to reject the pluralist position claiming the essential stability of Japanese politics. Foremost is the inference that the mainly centralized social and political institutions will be, indeed must be, redesigned to accommodate the more flexible requirements of a postindustrial Japan, where collective goods are coming to the fore (we shall see also whether the Japanese style of decision making offers special solutions to handle these new problems). This is so for several reasons. First, the growth of collective goods creates heightened mixes of incentives and sanctions that drive citizens into collective action. Who is this collective action directed at unless it is the government? From our perspective, it is unlikely that political participation itself will decline in Japanese society. It may well be the case that voting participation will decline, but we would expect to see evidence that local action groups and other "nonnormal" types of participation would increase substantially. Second, recently, Hirsch identified a new class of goods called positional goods. These are zero sum in nature: if I go to a national park in the Japan Alps to experience nature, I do not want you, the reader, there. The same point holds if I purchase my little vacation house in Karizawa. If Japan is moving into the postindustrial era, many more citizens than before have the material standard of living to pursue positional goods. If the above-mentioned point about economic growth slowdown has merit,

we then have the potential for many things in Japanese society becoming positional goods, for example, places at university, jobs,
and leadership positions throughout society. Conflict over positional goods is inevitable and intense. One can see evidence of the
rise of positional goods already. To go to certain rural regions of
Japan in the tourist season is not very pleasant. The examination
system that every Japanese must go through to enter university is
so intense that Japanese teen-agers commit suicide at greater rates
than any other age group in Japan. However, there is a last point,
abstracted from our discussion of the trends observed in postindustrial societies elsewhere, concerning the impact of value change.
If it is correct that the norm of equality diffuses throughout society,
it becomes increasingly difficult for advantaged classes to disallow
the claims of the minority groups in society; for their part, minority groups, including women here, will become more strident, as
they internalize the norm of equality themselves.

We should then find evidence of the redefinition of the limits
of Japanese politics. We present a table and a graph that contain
illustrative evidence—Table 6.2 on labor disputes and Figure 6.7
on local action interest groups (jyūmin undō). In fact, the image of
"Japan Incorporated" surely is inaccurate; the number of workers
involved in strikes and days lost doubled from 1965 to 1974. More
strikingly, we note the virtually exponential increase in local interest group activity over a 30-year postwar period.

TABLE 6.2

Labor Disputes: Work Stoppages in Industry, 1965-74

Year	Number of Disputes	Number of Involved	Days Lost (millions)
1965	1,542	1,682,342	5.669
1970	2,260	1,720,135	3.915
1974	5,211	3,621,049	9.663

Source: Sōrifu tōkeikyoku (Bureau of Statistics, Office of the
Prime Minister), Nihon tōkei nenkan [Japan statistical yearbook]
(Tokyo: Government Printing Office, 1975).

FIGURE 6.7

Growth of Jyumin Undō Movements (Local Interest Groups)

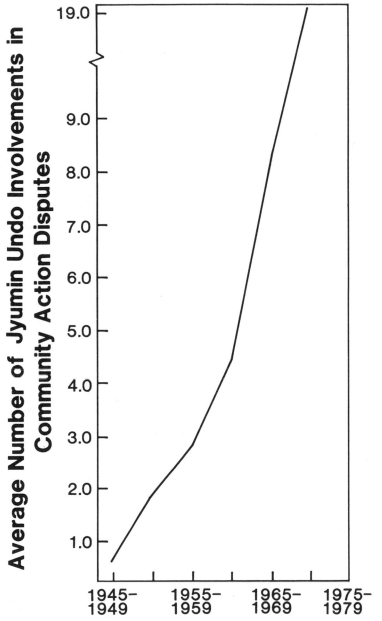

Source: Nihon sogo Kenkyujo, ed., Jyumin-sanka ni kansuru kenkyo (Tokyo: Shiryo-Hen, 1976).

The weak label placed on Japanese interest groups must be reconsidered. Politics is spilling out of "normal" channels of politics, and it is no longer accurate to place the compliant label on the Japanese public.

It is easy to see why many observers might be pessimistic about the future if one assumes that the present emphasis on centralization of political institutions is a requirement for political stability. We should not, however, ignore the rich Japanese cultural heritage, which includes strategies of decision making that might very well mitigate some of the negative dimensions of scenarios painted by observers of other postindustrial states.

THE FUTURE OF POLITICAL PARTIES

It is unlikely, in our judgment, that the Japanese political party system will be able to absorb the rise in political demands we have illustrated and predicted. These demands apparently flow around or over the party system directly to the more relevant bureaucratic structures. Certainly, in Japan, as elsewhere, voter turnout appears to be generally declining. It is the age of single-issue politics, and groups in Japanese society increasingly polarize around collective goods issues. Under such conditions, we may ask whether the Japanese political party system is in decline, or, in fact, whether it has a future. Indeed, this is a legitimate question—one asked in other postindustrial societies—and we end with our own projections.

We begin with our conclusion that political parties were developed in and for an industrial, not postindustrial, Japan. While the party system, however, has served its major role as a transmission belt of sorts between the elites and mass public, the Japanese political party system has always differed substantially from North American or Western European equivalents. In the West, parties, it is argued, have been the major arena through which interests have been aggregated and articulated, that is, where interest groups coalesced and transmitted their individual and joint demands to the government. Second, Western parties have traditionally been the vehicle through which national political leaders have been recruited. The party itself provided the ladder by which an ambitious individual climbed to the top. Third, parties in the West have traditionally helped shape national public policy by setting the agenda of public policy discussion for legislative bodies. It is questionable that Japanese parties have ever complied with this description. (It is, of course, now arguable whether their Western counterparts do.) This does not mean that the party system has been or is now a sterile force.

Japanese parties do not set the public policy agenda, but they remain a potent arena for policy debate and, through their Diet representatives, ratification of solutions proposed elsewhere (usually in the public bureaucracy). Personal support organizations, such as koenkai and habatsu, may be powerful political forces that engage in candidate selection and interest group articulation and aggregation. However, we have seen that these forces are, in fact, channeled through the party system. Moreover, all of these forces viewed as the institutionalized system of political demand channels, including the jyumin undō (local action) movements themselves, may prove very serviceable to meet the more complex and local-issue–dominated public issue agenda of the 1980s. This is so for several reasons. We begin with culture; we have emphasized the enduring strength of endogenous organization models; decision making from below (ringeisei), the rejection of the adversaried mode of decision making and emphasis on consensus; and the subordination of the individual within the group. If the postindustrial phase of sociopolitical change is to be the age of participation, these elements of the Japanese value system may very well be more adaptable to a changing world than value systems in the West. Second, while the Japanese have indeed industrialized over the past century, and consequently suffered from many negative externalities, such as pollution, their local communities remain largely in place. Unlike New York, for example, Tokyo is often described as 10,000 villages. Many urban residents still regard their rural village as their home. Japanese local communities have simply not experienced the level of disintegration that comparable communities in North America present. This local community base will provide a powerful anchor of stability in the face of the rise of political demands to come. Finally, whereas party systems elsewhere are apparently finding it difficult to survive and adapt to changing circumstances, the Japanese party system may already be largely congruent with the needs of a postindustrial world, in which political parties may well be only one of several types of political institutions used to make political demands and handle political conflict.

We, with many others, wonder about what would happen if and when the dominant LDP loses its hegemony, and a coalition, say, of opposition parties, takes over. The LDP remains resilient, but we suspect it will, at some point in the next several elections for the House of Representatives, lose power to such a coalition of opposition parties. We would make two projections about the implications of the scenario. The public, the public bureaucracy, and the business and labor interests can and will adapt, though there may well be debate and confusion. The larger point concerns the growing importance of the other political institutions and patterns we have referred to; if parties are not as crucial, political conflict over them is not likely to be as intense.

The Japanese face the same uncertain future that their sister postindustrial societies confront. Questions over the distribution of wealth, the growing irrelevance of neoclassical models in a service-, not industrial-, dominated economy, inflation, increasingly scarce energy and raw material resources, and solutions to collective goods problems exist; all told, these are daunting issues. Japan's largely centralized political institutions will, we project, undergo substantial redesign. Because of their history, the Japanese have, however, importantly different political resources than other postindustrial societies. These resources are the contextual values, the endogenous dimensions discussed here. Two values, consensus and participation, are crucial and perhaps worth studying closely by foreign counterparts, especially in postindustrial societies.

NOTES

1. Bradley M. Richardson, "Stability and Change in Japanese Voting Behavior," Journal of Asian Studies 36 (August 1977): 675-94; Scott Flanagan, "Value Change and Partisan Change in Japan: The Silent Revolution Revisited," Comparative Politics 2 (April 1979): 253-79; T. J. Pempel, "Political Parties and Social Change: The Japanese Experience," in Louis Maisel and Joseph Cooper, eds., Political Parties: Development and Decay (Beverly Hills, Calif.: Sage Publications, 1978), pp. 309-42.

2. The sketch that follows summarizes the argument developed in Roger Benjamin, The Limits of Politics: Collective Goods and Political Change in Postindustrial Societies (Chicago: University of Chicago Press, 1980). For another rational-choice-based study on Japan itself, see Nobutake Ike, A Theory of Japanese Democracy (Boulder, Colo.: Westview Press, 1978).

3. This indeed appears to be the case with Japan, as indicated in the excellent collection of studies in T. C. Pempel, ed., Policymaking in Contemporary Japan (Ithaca, N.Y.: Cornell University Press, 1977).

4. See Nobutake Ike, "Economic Growth and Intergenerational Change in Japan, American Political Science Review 7 (December 1973): 1194-203; Joji Watanuki, Politics in Postwar Japanese Society (Tokyo: Tokyo University Press, 1977).

5. Our source of data, summarized here, is the Institute of Statistical Mathematics, Office of the Prime Minister, Tokyo (in 1977).

6. Kasuto Kojima, "Public Opinion Trends in Japan," Public Opinion Quarterly 41 (Summer 1977): 211.

7. Jurgen Habermas, Legitimation Crisis (London: Heine-mann, 1976); Antonio Gramsci, Selections from Prison Notebooks, ed. and trans. Quintan Hoare and Geoffrey Nowell Smith (New York: International Publishers, 1971).

APPENDIX A:
PARTY BACKGROUND DATA

TABLE A.1

Number of Ex-bureaucrats Holding High Party Posts, 1955-74

Post	Total Number	Ex-bureaucrats	Percent
President	6	3	50.0
Vice-President	3	1	33.3
Secretary-General	9	3	33.3
Chair of the Executive Council	15	5	33.3
Chair of the Policy Affairs Research Council	17	7	41.2
Chair of the Finance Committee	12	6	50.0
Chair of the Organization Committee	14	3	21.4
Chair of the Publicity Committee	14	3	21.4
Chair of the Diet Policy Committee	18	2	11.1
Chair of the Party Discipline Committee	17	8	47.1
Total	90	30	33.3

Sources: Shugiin jimukyoku (House of Representatives Secretariat), Shugiin yōran [House of Representatives Survey] (Tokyo: Government Printing Office, 1955-72); Sangiin jimukyoku (House of Councillors Secretariat), Sangiin yōran [House of Councillors Survey] (Tokyo: Sangiin Jimukyoku, 1955-72); other data are with the courtesy of the Secretariat of the Liberal Democratic Party.

TABLE A.2

Sokagakkai Relationships of Komeito Members of the House of Representatives
and the House of Councillors, 1969

House of Representatives

Komeito Members	SG Position	Age	Party Position
Yoshikatsu Takeiri	Executive Director (Somu); Head of Tokyo 3rd District	37	Chair of the Party
Junya Yano	Vice-Chairman, Board of Trustees (Fuku-rijicho); Vice-Head, Tokyo 1st District	37	Secretary-General
Kiyoshi Ono	Vice-Chairman, Board of Trustees; Head of Santama 2d District	39	Vice-Secretary-General; Chair, Diet Affairs Committee
Koshiro Ishida	Executive Director	39	Head of the Komeito members of the House
Ichiro Watanabe	Vice-Chairman, Board of Trustees; Head of Hyogo 1st District	38	Vice-Secretary-General
Yoshiyuki Asai	Vice-Chairman, Board of Trustees; Head of Hyogo 4th District	42	Director, Policy Review Bureau
Kazuo Fushiki	Vice-Chairman, Board of Trustees; Head of Kanagawa 2d District	41	Vice-Chair, Diet Affairs Committee
Minoru Saito	Vice-Chairman, Board of Trustees; Head of Hokkaido 1st District	46	Vice-Chair, Diet Affairs Committee

Name		Age	
Yoshiaki Masaki	Trustee (Riji); Head of Sakai Branch	44	Vice-Chair, Diet Affairs Committee
Shinichiro Ogawa	Trustee; Head of Saitama 2d Branch	43	Vice-Director, Policy Bureau
Yasuo Suzukiri	Trustee; Head of Ota 2d Branch	43	Vice-Director Small–Medium Enterprises Bureau
Sosukemaru Ito	Trustee; Head of Narima Branch	36	Vice-Director, Policy Bureau
Shigetake Arishima	Trustee; Vice-Head of Koto 1st Branch	45	Vice-Director, Social Welfare Bureau
Chusuke Matsumoto	Trustee; Head of Arakawa 1st Branch	55	Vice-Director, Labor Bureau
Shinji Kohama	Trustee' Head of Kanagawa 3rd District	54	Vice-Director, Youth Bureau
Shinichi Higami	Trustee; Head of Kyoto 1st Branch	62	Vice-Director, Social Welfare Bureau
Yasuyuki Okimoto	Trustee; Vice-Head of Kansai 1st District	49	Vice-Director, Labor Bureau
Miki Omi	Trustee; Vice-Director Youth Director	34	Central Executive Committee Member
Giichi Kitagawa	Trustee; Head of (Kansai) Ikuno Branch	42	Vice-Director, Small–Medium Enterprises Bureau
Tomio Okamoto	Trustee; Vice-Head of Hyogo 1st District	48	Vice-Director, Public Relation Bureau
Taro Yamada	Vice-Chair, Board of Trustees; Head of Chugoku 2d District	51	Vice-Director, Education Bureau

(continued)

Table A.2, continued

Komeito Members	SG Position	Age	Party Position
Naoki Hirosawa	Trustee; Head of Hiroshima Branch	38	Director, Labor Bureau
Akira Nakano	Trustee; Vice-Head of Shikoku District	43	Vice-Director, Agriculture, Forestry and Fishery Bureau
Shoji Tanaka	Trustee; Head of Fukuoka 3rd Branch	42	Vice-Director, Agriculture, Forestry and Fishery Bureau
Toshio Ohashi	Vice-Chair, Board of Trustees; Head of Kitakyushu District	44	Vice-Director, Youth Bureau
House of Councillors			
Hiroshi Hojo	Executive Director (Somu), Head of Tokyo 1st District	46	Vice-Chair of the Party
Giichiro Shiraki	Executive Director; Head of Kansai 1st District	50	Vice-Chair of the Party
Kazuhiro Suzuki	Executive Director; Head of Saitama District	45	Director, Policy Bureau
Kunihiko Shibuya	Vice-Chair, Board of Trustees (Fuku-rijicho); Head of Aichi 2d District	45	Vice-Secretary-General
Akira Kuroyanagi	Vice-Chair, Board of Trustees; Vice-Head of Tokyo 8th District	38	Vice-Secretary-General

148

Name	Position/District	Age	Title
Bunzo Ninomiya	Executive Director; Head of Shikoku District	49	Director, International Affairs Bureau
Shogo Tada	Executive Director; Head of Tokyo 8th District	38	Vice-Secretary-General
Yoshihei Kodaira	Executive Director; Director of Religious Instruction	48	Head of the Komeito Members of the House of Councillors
Fujio Tashiro	Executive Director; Head of Kansai 2d District	38	Director, Organization Bureau
Yasu Kashiwabara	Executive Director; Director of Women Department	52	Director, Women's Bureau
Hidehiko Yaoi	Executive Director; Head of Kansai 3rd District	36	Director, Students' Bureau
Tatsuyoshi Nakao	Trustee (Riji); Vice-Head of Kyoto District	53	Vice-Director, Diet Affairs
Teruichi Yamada	Executive Director; Head of Chugoku 1st District	48	Chair, Party Discipline Committee
Tatsuru Harada	Executive Director; Head of Kyushu 1st District	43	Vice-Director, Organization Bureau
Masayoshi Miyazaki	Executive Director; Head of Kokkaido 2d District	57	Director, Agriculture, Forestry and Fishery Bureau
Toru Asai	Vice-Chair, Board of Trustees; Head of Hyogo 2d District	67	Director, National Medical Treatment Bureau

(continued)

Table A.2, continued

Komeito Members	SG Position	Age	Party Position
Kenichi Abe	Member	60	Director, Tokyo Federation of the Komeito
Zenri Uchida	Vice-Chair, Board of Trustees	51	Director, Land Development Bureau
Minoru Sawada	Vice-Chair, Board of Trustees	46	Secretary-General of the Gifu Federation of the Komeito
Keisuke Shiode	Vice-Chair, Board of Trustees	36	Director, Social Welfare Bureau
Fusao Fujiwara	Vice-Chair, Board of Trustees; Secretary-General of the Hokkaido District	40	Director, Disease Prevention Bureau
Takao Miki	Executive Director; Vice-Director of Youth Department	34	Director, Youth Bureau
Akinori Mineyama	Vice-Chair, Board of Trustees; Secretary-General of Kansai District	34	Director, City Bureau
Shigejiro Kanbayashi	Vice-Chair, Board of Trustees	52	Director, National Life Bureau

Sources: Shugiin jimukyoku (House of Representatives Secretariat), Shugiin yōran [House of Representatives Survey] (Tokyo: Government Printing Office, 1967); Sangiin jimukyoku (House of Councillors Secretariat), Sangiin yōran [House of Councillors Survey] (Tokyo: Government Printing Office, 1968); Hisashi Nishijima, Komeitō [Clean Government Party] (Tokyo: Sekkasha, 1968), pp. 166–89.

APPENDIX B:
FACTION MEMBERSHIP

Prime Minister	Faction Membership N	Cabinet Ministers N
1958		
Kishi	54	5
Sato	36	3
Kono	33	2
Ono	37	2
Ikeda	33	1
Miki/Matumura	34	1
Ishii	22	1
Ishibashi	14	0
Total: 8 factions	263	
Double membership	24	1
Independents	11	0
Total	298	16
1958-6-12		
Kishi Cabinet (2nd)		
1960		
Ikeda	49	6
Kishi	45	3
Sato	44	2
Fujiyama	26	1
Kono	32	1
Ono	26	1
Miki/Matsumura	25	1
Ishii	18	0
Total: 8 factions	265	
Double membership	22	0
Independents	12	1
Total	299	16
1960-12-8		
Ikeda (2nd Cabinet)		
1962		
Ikeda	51	5
Sato	52	2
Kishi	49	2

(continued)

Prime Minister	Faction Membership N	Cabinet Ministers N
Fujiyama	28	1
Kono	31	2
Ono	30	2
Miki/Matsumura	33	1
Ishii	14	1
Ishibashi	4	0
Ishida	4	0
Total: 10 factions	296	
Independents	2	0
Total	299	16

1962-7-18
Ikeda Cabinet (2nd)

1963

	Faction Membership N	Cabinet Ministers N
Ikeda	50	4
Sato	49	2
Sashin-renmei (Fukuda)	21 (adjusted)	0
Koyu-Club (Kawashima)	25	2
Kishi-related	4	0
Kaya-related	3	1
Fujiyama	24	1
Kono	31	2
Ono	29	2
Miki/Matsumura	32	1
Ishii	14	1
Ishibashi	4	0
Ishida	4	0
Total: 13 factions	290	
Independents	2	0
Total	292	16

1963-12-9
Ikeda Cabinet (3rd)

1964

	Faction Membership N	Cabinet Ministers N
Ikeda	49	4
Sato	46	2
Kono	48	2

Prime Minister	Faction Membership N	Cabinet Ministers N
Miki	37	2
Ono	30	2
(Tofu) Sashin-renmei (Fukuda)	21	0
Fujiyama	21	1
Koyu-Club (Kawashima)	19	2
Ishii	14	0
Total: 9 factions	285	
Independents	15	1
Total	300	16

1964-7-18
Ikeda Cabinet (3rd)

1965

Ikeda	49	2
Sato	44	4
Kono	47	1
Miki	37	2
Old Ono	26	2
(Tofu) Sashin-renmei (Fukuda)	19	0
Fujiyama	20	1
Koyu-Club (Kawashima)	17	2
Ishii	13	0
Total: 9 factions	272	
Independents	18	1
Total	290	15

1964-11-9
Sato Cabinet (1st)

1966

Old Ikeda	47	2
Sato	44	5
Old Kono	45	1
Miki	36	2
Funada	13	0
Murakami	11	1
Fukuda	19	2
Fujiyama	18	1

(continued)

Prime Minister	Faction Membership N	Cabinet Ministers N
Koyu-Club (Kawashima)	17	1
Ishii	13	1
Total: 10 factions	263	
Independents	20	0
Total	283	16
1965-6-3		
Sato Cabinet		

1967

Sato	57	6
Old Ikeda	42	2
Miki	36	3
Fukuda	23	2
Nakasone	24	0
Kawashima	18	1
Fujiyama	17	0
Funada	15	1
Mori	14	0
Ishii	14	1
Murakami	10	0
Matsumura	4	0
Total: 12 factions	274	
Independents	11	0
Total	285	16
1967-2-17		
Sato Cabinet		

1968

Sato	57	6
Old Ikeda	42	2
Miki	35	2
Fukuda	23	1
Nakasone	24	1
Kawashima	17	1
Fujiyama	17	0
Funada	15	1
Mori	14	1
Ishii	13	1

Prime Minister	Faction Membership N	Cabinet Ministers N
Murakami	10	0
Matsumura	4	0
Total: 12 factions	271	
Independents	11	0
Total	282	16

1967-11-25
Sato Cabinet (2nd)

1969

Sato	54	4
Maeo	43	2
Miki	37	2
Fukuda	28	2
Nakasone	25	1
Kawashima	17	1
Funada	13	1
Ishii	13	1
Fujiyama	7	0
Old Mori	10	0
Murakami	10	1
Nanjo	6	1
Matsumura	4	0
Total: 13 factions	267	
Independents	8	0
Total	275	16

1968-11-30
Sato Cabinet (2nd)

1970

Sato	59	4
Maeo	44	3
Miki	42	2
Fukuda	36	2
Nakasone	36	2
Kawashima	19	1
Funada	13	0
Sonoda	12	1

(continued)

Prime Minister	Faction Membership N	Cabinet Ministers N
Ishii	13	1
Murakami	10	0
Ishida	6	0
Fujiyama	6	0
Old Matsumura	2	0
Total: 13 factions	298	
Independents	5	0
Total	303	16
1970-1-14		
Sato Cabinet (3rd)		

1971

Prime Minister	Faction Membership N	Cabinet Ministers N
Sato	60	4
Maeo	43	3
Miki	42	2
Fukuda	37	2
Nakasone	36	2
Shiina	18	1
Funada	13	0
Sonoda	12	1
Ishii	13	1
Murakami	10	0
Ishida	6	0
Fujiyama	6	0
Old Matsumura	2	0
Total: 13 factions	298	
Independents	5	0
Total	303	16
1970-1-14		
Sato Cabinet (3rd)		
(also Kokkai-benran		
2-1-71)		

Prime Minister	Faction Membership in the H. of R. N	Faction-related Membership in the H. of C.* N	Total N
1972 (S. 47)			
Sato	61	44	105
Ohira	43	16	59
Miki	45	12	57
Fukuda	38	19	57
Nakasone	34	7	41
Shiina	17	4	21
Mizuta	16	3	19
Sonoda	12	0	12
Ishii	13	0	13
Funada	12	4	16
Fujiyama	3	0	3
Old Matsumura	3	0	3
		8 faction-related	
Total: 12 factions	297	109	406
Independents	5	24	
Total	302	133	
1973 (S. 48)			
Fukuda	56	29	85
Tanaka	48	39	87
Ohira	45	20	65
Miki	37	11	48
Nakasone	36	6	42
Shiina	18	4	22
Mizuta	13	2	15
Funada	12	4	16
Ishii	10	5	15
		9 faction-related	
Total: 9 factions	275	120	395
Independents	13	16	
Total	288	136	

*All are "faction-related."

(continued)

Prime Minister	Faction Membership in the H. of R. N	Faction-related Membership in the H. of C.* N	Total N
1974 (S. 49)			
Fukuda	56	27	83
Tanaka	47	39	86
Ohira	42	20	62
Miki	37	11	48
Nakasone	36	6	42
Shiina	18	4	22
Mizuta	13	2	15
Funada	9	4	13
Ishii	9	5	14
		9 faction-related	
Total: 9 factions	267	118	385
Independents	14	16	
Total	281	134	
1975 (S. 50)			
Fukuda	56	23	79
Tanaka	47	43	90
Ohira	42	21	63
Miki	36	10	46
Nakasone	35	5	40
Shiina	18	2	20
Mizuta	12	2	14
Funada	8	3	11
Ishii	8	0	8
		8 faction-related	
Total: 9 factions	262	109	371
Independents	18	19	
Total	280	128	

*All are "faction-related."

Prime Minister	Faction Membership in the H. of R. N	Faction-related Membership in the H. of C.* N	Total N
1976 (S. 51)			
Fukuda	55	23	78
Tanaka	49	44	93
Ohira	43	20	63
Miki	36	10	46
Nakasone	35	5	40
Shiina	17	2	19
Mizuta	11	2	13
Funada	8	3	11
Ishii	6	0	6
	8 faction-related		
Total: 9 factions	260	109	369
Independents	14	19	
Total	274	128	
1977 (As of 12-8-76 after the 12-5-76 H. of R. election)			
Fukuda	54	22	75
Tanaka (old)	46	41	86
Ohira	38	20	58
Nakasone	38	5	42
Miki	32	10	42
Shiina	11	2	13
Mizuta	10	2	13
Funada	8	3	11
Ishii	4	0	4
	8 faction-related		
Total: 9 factions	239	105	344
Independents	19	20	
Total	260	125	

*All but the old-Tanaka faction are "faction-related."

Sources: Compiled by Kan Ori based on the data from the Asahi shimbun [Asahi newspaper], December 7 and 8, 1976; Kokkai binran [Diet handbook] of August 1, 1976 (Tokyo: Nihon Seikei Shimbun Shuppanbu, 1976), and the N.H.K. news reporting of December 6, 1976.

APPENDIX C:
VARIABLE IDENTIFICATION

1. POLITICAL PARTY IDENTIFICATION

   ____Liberal Democratic Party
   ____Japan Socialist Party
   ____Democratic Socialist Party
   ____Komei Party
   ____Japan Communist Party
   ____Independents
   ____Not available

2. AGE

   ____Below 35
   ____36-45
   ____46-55
   ____56-65
   ____66 and over

3. NUMBER OF TIMES ELECTED TO PREFECTURAL ASSEMBLY

   ____1
   ____2-3
   ____4-5
   ____6 times or more

4. FATHER'S OCCUPATION

   ____Small-, medium-sized businessmen
   ____Farmers and fishermen
   ____Blue-collar workers
   ____White-collar workers
   ____Public officials
   ____Others
   ____Not available

5. OCCUPATION

   ____Small-, medium-sized businessmen
   ____Farmers and fishermen
   ____Labor union and/or labor-related organization executives
   ____White-collar workers
   ____Public officials
   ____Secretaries of the Diet members
   ____Professionals
   ____Others (nonlabor organization executives, etc.)
   ____Not available.

6. ORGANIZATIONAL EXECUTIVE POST

_____Labor-related organizations
_____Farm-related organizations
_____Business and professional organizations
_____Local organizations
_____Others
_____Not available

7. RELATIVE'S PUBLIC OFFICE EXPERIENCE

_____Yes
_____No
_____Not available

8. PUBLIC OFFICE EXPERIENCE

_____Local legislative
_____Local executive
_____Local legislative-local executive
_____Local legislative-city legislative
_____City legislative
_____City legislative-city executive
_____Others
_____Nonpublic office experience
_____Not available

9. POLITICAL PARTY POST EXPERIENCE
(highest party post achieved)

_____Local level official
_____Prefectural level official
_____National party headquarters official
_____None
_____Not available

10. LEGISLATIVE LEADERSHIP POST EXPERIENCE
(House Speakership)

_____Yes
_____No

11. NUMBER OF CANDIDATES PER DISTRICT FROM THE
SAME PARTY

_____1
_____2
_____3 and more
_____Not available

12. POLITICAL AMBITION ("Do you consider the present post as your last public office?")

    ____Yes (no political ambition)
    ____No (political ambition)
    ____Maybe (latent political ambition)
    ____Japan Communist Party bases
    ____Not available

13. IMPORTANCE OF PRESENT POST FOR THE ATTAINMENT OF OTHER PUBLIC OFFICES IN THE FUTURE

    ____Yes
    ____Maybe
    ____No
    ____Not available

14. RANKED IMPORTANCE OF FACTORS IDENTIFIED AS THE CHIEF DETERMINANT IN THE ELECTION

    ____Koenkai
    ____Faction
    ____Party
    ____Koenkai-party
    ____Koenkai-faction
    ____Not available

GLOSSARY

Buraku	hamlet
Daimyo	feudal lords
Domei	Japanese Confederation of Labor
Habatsu	factions
Horei	statutes and ordinances
Jiyuminshuto	Liberal Democratic Party
Jiyuto	Liberal Party
Jyumin undō	local action interest groups
Kaishinto	Progressive Party
Koenkai	personal support organization (of individual legislators)
Kokuminkyodoto	People's Co-operative Party
Kokuminkyokai (Kokuminseijikyokai)	People's (Political) Association, a fund-channeling organization of the Liberal Democratic Party
Kokuminminshuto	People's Democratic Party
Kokuminseito	a people's party (not a party of a class)
Kokuminto	People's Party
Komeito	Clean Government Party (Fair Play Party)
Kyosanto	Communist Party
Minseito	Popular Government Party (Progressive Party), a prewar conservative party
Minshato (Minshushakaito)	Democratic Socialist Party
Minshujiyuto	Democratic Liberal Party
Nichiren-shoshu	Nichiren sect of Japanese Buddhism

Nihonjiyuto	Japan Liberal Party
Nihonkyodoto	Japan Co-operative Party
Nihonkyosanto	Japan Communist Party
Nihonminshuto	Japan Democratic Party
Nihonrodoto	Japan Labor Party
Nihonshakaito	Japan Socialist Party
Nihonshakaito-saha	Japan Socialist Party-Left
Nihonshakaito-uha	Japan Socialist Party-Right
Nihonshimpoto	Japan Progressive Party
Oyabun-kobun	parent-child role
Ringeisei	decision making from below
Rodonominto	Labor Farmer Party (a prewar socialist party)
Sashin-renmei	Renewal League (the Fukuda faction of the Liberal Democratic Party)
Seimuchosakai	Policy Affairs Research Council (of the Liberal Democratic Party)
Seiyukai	Political Friends (Liberal Party), a prewar conservative party
Shakaiminshuto	Socialist Democratic Party
Sohyo	General Council of Trade Unions of Japan
Sokagakkai	Value Creation Society, the Nichiren-shoshu sect of Buddhist lay group
Tatoka	a trend toward a multiparty pattern

BIBLIOGRAPHY

ENGLISH LANGUAGE SOURCES

Almond, Gabriel, and G. Bingham Powell. Comparative Politics: A Developmental Approach. Boston: Little, Brown, 1967.

Almond, Gabriel, and Sidney Verba. The Civic Culture. Princeton, N.J.: Princeton University Press, 1963.

Althauser, Robert P. "Multicollinearity and Non-additive Regression Models." In Causal Models in the Social Sciences, edited by Herbert M. Blalock, Jr., pp. 453-72. Chicago: Aldine-Atherton, 1971.

Apter, David E. The Politics of Modernization. Chicago: University of Chicago Press, 1965.

Baerwald, Hans H. "Factional Politics in Japan." Current History 46 (April 1964): 223-29, 243-44.

_____. "Japan: 'Black Mist' and Pre-Electioneering." Asian Survey 7 (January 1967): 31-39.

_____. "Japan at Election Time." Asian Survey 5 (January 1966): 646-55.

_____. "Japan: New Diplomatic Horizons, Old-Style Domestic Politics." Asian Survey 8 (January 1968): 43-51.

_____. "Japan: The Politics of Transition." Asian Survey 5 (January 1965): 33-42.

Beckmann, George M., and Okubo Genji. The Japanese Communist Party. Stanford, Calif.: Stanford University Press, 1969.

Belloni, Frank, and Dennis C. Bellehedal, eds. Factions and Parties. Santa Barbara, Calif.: ABC-Clio Press, 1978.

Benjamin, Roger. The Limits of Politics: Collective Goods and Political Change in Postindustrial Societies. Chicago: University of Chicago Press, 1980.

_____. "Minerva and the Crane (Tsuru): Birds of a Feather? Comparative Research and Japanese Political Change." Journal of Asian Studies (November 1930): 69-77.

Benjamin, Roger, Alan Arian, Richard N. Blue, and Steve Coleman. Patterns of Political Development: Japan, India, Israel. New York: David McKay, 1972.

Benjamin, Roger, and John H. Kautsky. "Communism and Economic Development." American Political Science Review 62 (March 1968): 131-44.

Brass, Paul. Factional Politics in an Indian State: The Congress Party in Uttar Pradesh. Berkeley and Los Angeles: University of California Press, 1965.

Brunner, Ronald D., and Klaus Liepelt. "Data Analysis, Process Analysis, and System Change." Midwest Journal of Political Science 16 (November 1972): 538-69.

Brzezinski, Zbigniew. The Fragile Blossom. New York: Harper & Row, 1972.

Buchanan, James, and Gorden Tullock. The Calculus of Consent. Ann Arbor: University of Michigan Press, 1961.

Choi, Sung-il. "Systems Outputs, Social Environment, and Political Cleavages in Japan: The Case of the 1969 General Election." American Journal of Political Science 18 (February 1973): 99-122.

Cole, Allan B., George O. Totten, and Cecil R. Uyehara. Socialist Parties in Postwar Japan. New Haven, Conn.: Yale University Press, 1966.

Cole, Robert. Japanese Blue Collar: The Changing Tradition. Berkeley and Los Angeles: University of California Press, 1971.

Coleman, Steve. Measurement and the Analysis of Political Systems. New York: John Wiley, 1975.

Curtis, Gerald L. Election Campaigning Japanese Style. New York: Columbia University Press, 1971.

Davis, M. D. Game Theory. New York: Basic Books, 1970.

Deutsch, Karl W. Nationalism and Social Communication. Cambridge, Mass.: M.I.T. Press, 1966.

_____. "Social Mobilization and Political Development." American Political Science Review 55 (September 1961): 493-514.

Duus, Peter. Party Rivalry and Political Change in Taisho Japan. Cambridge, Mass.: Harvard University Press, 1968.

Eisenstadt, S. N. Tradition, Change, and Modernity. New York: John Wiley, 1973.

Emi, Koichi. Government Fiscal Activity and Economic Growth in Japan, 1868-1960. Tokyo: Kinokuniya Bookstore, 1963.

Fahs, Charles B. Government in Japan: Recent Trends in Its Scope and Organization. New York: Institute of Pacific Relations, 1940.

Farnsworth, Lee W. "Challenges to Factionalism in Japan's Liberal Democratic Party." Asian Survey 6 (September 1966): 501-9.

_____. "Social and Political Sources of Political Fragmentation in Japan." Journal of Politics 29 (May 1967): 287-301.

Flanagan, Scott. "The Japanese Party System in Transition." Comparative Politics 3 (January 1971): 231-53.

_____. "Value Change and Partisan Change in Japan: The Silent Revolution Revisited." Comparative Politics 2 (April 1979): 253-79.

Friedrich, Carl J. Man and His Government: An Empirical Theory of Politics. New York: McGraw-Hill, 1963.

Frolich, Norman, Joe Oppenheimer, and Oran Young. Political Leadership and Collective Goods. Princeton, N.J.: Princeton University Press, 1971.

Fukui, Haruhiro. "The Associational Basis of Decision-Making in the Liberal Democratic Party." In Papers on Modern Japan, pp. 18-33. Canberra, Australia: Research School of Pacific Studies, Institute of Advanced Studies, 1965.

_____. "Factionalism in a Dominant Party System: The Case of Japan." In Faction Politics, edited by Frank P. Belloni and Dennis C. Beller. Santa Barbara, Calif.: ABC-Clio Press, 1978.

_____. Party in Power. Berkeley: University of California Press, 1970.

Goodenough, Ward. Description and Comparison in Cultural Anthropology. Chicago: Aldine, 1970.

Graham, B. D. "The Succession of Factional Systems in the Uttar Pradesh Congress Party, 1937-66." In Local-Level Politics, edited by Marc J. Swartz. Chicago: Aldine Publishing, 1968.

Gramsci, Antonio. Selections from Prison Notebooks. Edited and translated by Quintan Hoare and Geoffrey Nowell Smith. New York: International Publishers, 1971.

Gusfield, Joseph R. "Tradition and Modernity: Misplaced Polarities in the Study of Social Change." American Journal of Sociology 72 (January 1967): 351-62.

Habermas, Jurgen. Legitimation Crisis. London: Heinemann, 1976.

Harsanyi, John C. "Rational-Choice Models of Political Behavior vs. Functionalist and Conformist Theories." World Politics 2 (July 1969): 91-108.

Hellman, Donald. China and Japan: A New Balance of Power. Lexington, Mass.: Lexington Books, 1976.

Hempel, Carl G. "The Logic of Functional Analysis." In Symposium on Sociological Theory, edited by Llewellyn Gross, pp. 207-307. Evanston, Ill.: Row, Peterson, 1959.

Hirsch, Fred. The Social Limits to Growth. Cambridge, Mass.: Harvard University Press, 1976.

Huntington, Samuel P. "The Change to Change: Modernization, Development, and Politics." Comparative Politics 3 (April 1971): 283-322.

_____. "Political Development and Political Decay." World Politics 17 (April 1965): 386–411.

_____. Political Order in Changing Societies. New Haven, Conn.: Yale University Press, 1968.

_____. "Postindustrial Politics: How Benign Will It Be?" Comparative Politics 6 (January 1974): 163–91.

Ike, Nobutake. The Beginning of Political Democracy in Japan. Baltimore, Md.: Johns Hopkins Press, 1950.

_____. "Economic Growth and Intergenerational Change in Japan." American Political Science Review 67 (December 1973): 1194–203.

_____. A Theory of Japanese Democracy. Boulder, Colo. Westview Press, 1978.

Institute of International Relations. Survey. Tokyo: Institute of International Relations, Sophia University, 1972.

Ishida, Takeshi. Japanese Society. Boston: Random House, 1972.

Janda, Kenneth. A Conceptual Framework for the Comparative Analysis of Political Parties. Comparative Politics Series, vol. 1. Beverly Hills, Calif.: Sage Publications, 1970.

Johnston, Scott D. "A Comparative Study of Intra-Party Factionalism in Israel and Japan." The Western Political Science Quarterly 20 (June 1967): 288–307.

Kahn, Herman. The Emerging Japanese Super State: Challenge and Response. Englewood Cliffs, N.J.: Prentice-Hall, 1970.

Kamo, H. "Empirical Studies of the JSP Factions." Monograph Series, no. 5. Tokyo: Japan Institute of Political Studies, 1975.

Karsh, Bernard, and Robert E. Cole. "Industrialization and the Convergence Hypothesis: Some Aspects of Contemporary Japan." Journal of Social Issues 24 (October 1968): 45–64.

Kasahara, Kazuo. "Soka Gakkai and Komeito." Japan Quarterly 14 (March 1967): 311–20.

Keohane, Robert O. "Institutionalization in the United Nations' General Assembly." International Organization 23 (Autumn 1969): 859-96.

Kesselman, Mark J. "Change in the French Party System." Comparative Politics 4 (January 1972): 281-301.

Kim, Chong Lim. "Socio-Economic Development and Political Democracy in Japanese Prefectures." American Political Science Review 65 (March 1971): 184-86.

Kojima, Kasuto. "Public Opinion Trends in Japan." Public Opinion Quarterly 41 (Summer 1977): 208-21.

Kyogoku, Junichi, and Nobutaka Ike. "Urban-rural Differences in Voting Behavior in Postwar Japan." The Proceedings of the Department of Social Sciences, no. 9. Tokyo: University of Tokyo, College of General Education, 1959.

Lande, Carl. Leaders, Factions, and Parties: The Structure of Philippine Politics. Southeast Asian Studies, Monograph Series, no. 6. New Haven, Conn.: Yale University Press, 1965.

Langdon, Frank C. "Japanese Liberal Democratic Factional Discord on China Policy." Pacific Affairs 41 (Fall 1968): 403-15.

_____. "The Political Contributions of Big Business in Japan." Asian Survey 3 (October 1963): 465-73.

_____. Politics in Japan. Boston: Little, Brown, 1967.

Langer, Paul F. Communism in Japan. Stanford, Calif.: Hoover Institution Press, 1972.

Leiserson, Michael. "Factions and Coalitions in One-Party Japan: An Interpretation Based on the Theory of Games." American Political Science Review 62 (September 1968): 770-87.

Lipset, S. M. Political Man. New York: Doubleday, 1961.

_____. "Some Social Requisites of Democracy: Economic Development and Political Legitimacy." American Political Science Review 53 (March 1959): 69-105.

Masumi, Junnosuke. "A Profile of the Japanese Conservative Party." Asian Survey 3 (August 1963): 390–401.

Michels, Robert. Political Parties. New York: Collier Books, 1962.

Milbrath, Lester. Political Participation. Chicago: Rand McNally, 1977.

Moore, Barrington. The Social Origins of Democracy and Dictatorship. Boston: Beacon Press, 1966.

Najita, Tetsou. Hara Kei and the Politics of Compromise. Cambridge, Mass.: Harvard University Press, 1967.

Nakane, Chie. Japanese Society. Berkeley and Los Angeles: University of California Press, 1971.

Nicholas, Ralph. "Village Factions and Political Parties in Rural West Bengal." Journal of Commonwealth Political Studies 2 (March 1963): 17–32.

Ohkawa, Kayushi. The Growth Rate of the Japanese Economy Since 1878. Tokyo: Kinokuniya Bookstore, 1957.

Olson, Mancur, Jr. The Logic of Collective Action. Cambridge, Mass.: Harvard University Press, 1965.

Ori, Kan. "The Japanese Higher Bureaucracy." Paper presented to the International Management Development Seminar, September 1969, Tokyo. Mimeographed.

Ortega y Gasset, Jose. The Revolt of the Masses. New York: W. W. Norton, 1957.

Passin, Herbert. Society and Education in Japan. New York: Columbia University Press, 1965.

Pempel, T. J. "The Bureaucratization of Policymaking in Postwar Japan." American Journal of Political Science 18 (November 1974): 647–64.

_____. "Japanese Foreign Economic Policy: The Domestic Basis for International Behavior." International Organization 31 (Autumn 1977): 723–74.

_____, ed. Policymaking in Contemporary Japan. Ithaca, N.Y.: Cornell University Press, 1977.

_____. "Political Parties and Social Change: The Japanese Experience." In Political Parties: Development and Decay, edited by M. Louis Maisel and Joseph Cooper, pp. 309-42. Beverly Hills, Calif.: Sage Publications, 1978.

Polsby, Nelson W. "The Institutionalization of the United States House of Representatives." American Political Science Review 62 (March 1968): 148-68.

Prewitt, Kenneth. "Political Ambitions, Volunteerism, and Electoral Accountability." American Political Science Review 64 (March 1970): 5-17.

_____. The Recruitment of Political Leaders: A Study of Citizen-Politicians. Indianapolis, Ind.: Bobbs-Merrill, 1970.

Przeworski, Adam, and John D. Sprague. "Concepts in Search of Explicit Formulation: A Study in Measurement." Midwest Journal of Political Science 15 (May 1971): 183-218.

Przeworski, Adam, and Henry Teune. The Logic of Comparative Social Inquiry. New York: John Wiley, 1969.

Rae, Douglas W., Jr. The Political Consequences of Electoral Laws. New Haven, Conn.: Yale University Press, 1971.

Reischauer, Edwin O. The Japanese. Cambridge, Mass.: The Belknap Press, 1977.

Richardson, Bradley M. The Political Culture of Japan. Berkeley and Los Angeles: University of California Press, 1973.

_____. "Stability and Change in Japanese Voting Behavior." Journal of Asian Studies 36 (August 1977): 675-94.

_____. "Urbanization and Political Participation: The Case of Japan." American Political Science Review 67 (June 1973): 433-52.

Scalapino, Robert A. Democracy and the Party Movement in Prewar Japan: The Failure of the First Attempt. Berkeley and Los Angeles: University of California Press, 1953.

Scalapino, Robert A., and Junnosuke Masumi. The Japanese Communist Movement, 1920-1966. Berkeley and Los Angeles: University of California Press, 1976.

_____. Parties and Politics in Contemporary Japan. Berkeley and
Los Angeles: University of California Press, 1962.

Schlesinger, Joseph A. Ambition and Politics. Chicago: Rand
McNally, 1966.

Schmitter, Phillippe C. "Still the Century of Corporatism?" In
The New Corporatism, edited by Frederick B. Pike and Thomas
Stritch, pp. 85-131. Notre Dame, Ind.: University of Notre
Dame Press, 1974.

Shinoda, Yujiro. "Management Associations and Government Agencies in Japan." Vol. 1. Tokyo: Sophia University Socio-
Economic Institute, 1967. Mimeographed.

Shinohara, Hajime, and Yoshinori Ide. "Images of Election Held by
the Successful Candidates: The Case of Japan in 1967." Paper
presented at the meeting of 7th International Political Science
Association Congress, August 1967, Brussels, Belgium. Mimeographed.

Shively, W. Phillips. "Voting Stability and the Nature of Party
Attachments in the Weimar Republic." American Political
Science Review 66 (December 1972): 1203-25.

Silberman, Bernard. "Ringisei—Traditional Values or Organizational Imperatives in the Japanese Upper Civil Service: 1868-
1945." Journal of Asian Studies 32 (February 1973): 251-64.

Sorauf, Frank J. Political Parties in the American System. Boston:
Little, Brown, 1964.

Soukup, James R. "Japan, Comparative Political Finance: A Symposium." Journal of Politics 25 (August 1963): 737-56.

Stockwin, J. A. "Factions and Ideology in Postwar Japanese Socialism." In Papers on Modern Japan, pp. 34-49. Canberra,
Australia: Research School of Pacific Studies, Institute of Advanced Studies, 1965.

Sugimori, Koji. "Social Background of Political Leadership in
Japan." The Developing Economies 6 (December 1968): 34-59.

Thayer, N. B. "Elections, Coalitions, and Prime Ministery in Japan 1976-1985." In Japan: The Paradox of Progress, edited by Lewis Austin, pp. 11-31. New Haven, Conn.: Yale University Press, 1976.

_____. How the Conservatives Rule Japan. Princeton, N.J.: Princeton University Press, 1969.

Totten, George O. "Recent Factional Developments in the Japan Socialist Party: The Rise of New Types of Factions." Paper presented at the annual meeting of International Studies Association, February 1976, Toronto, Canada. Mimeographed.

Totten, George O., and Tamio Kawakami. "The Functions of Factionalism in Japanese Politics." Pacific Affairs 38 (Summer 1965): 109-22.

Tsurutani, Taketsugu. Political Change in Japan: Response to Postindustrial Challenge. New York: Longman, 1977.

Vogel, Ezra. Japan as Number One: Lessons for America. Cambridge, Mass.: Harvard University Press, 1979.

Ward, Robert E. Japan's Political System. 2d ed. Englewood Cliffs, N.J.: Prentice-Hall, 1978.

_____, ed. Political Development in Modern Japan. Princeton, N.J.: Princeton University Press, 1965.

_____. "Urban-Rural Differences and the Process of Political Modernization in Japan: A Case Study." Economic Development and Cultural Change 9 (October 1960).

Watanuki, Joji. Politics in Postwar Japanese Society. Tokyo: Tokyo University Press, 1977.

_____. "Social Structure and Political Participation in Japan." Tokyo: Institute of International Relations, Sophia University, 1972. Mimeographed.

Weinberg, Ian. "The Problems of the Convergence of Industrial Societies: A Critical Look at the State of a Theory." Comparative Studies in Society and History 11 (January 1969): 1-15.

White, James W. Sokagakkai: The Politics of Mass Society. Stanford, Calif.: Stanford University Press, 1971.

_____. "Tradition and Politics in Studies of Contemporary Japan." World Politics 26 (April 1974): 400-27.

JAPANESE LANGUAGE SOURCES

Asahi janaru [Asahi journal]. A weekly magazine. Tokyo: Asahi shimbunsha.

Asahi nenkan [Asahi yearbook]. Tokyo shimbunsha, 1974.

Asahi Shimbun, ed. Seitō to habatsu [Political parties and factions]. Tokyo: Asahi Shimbunsha, 1968.

Chūō Kōron [The central review]. A monthly magazine. Tokyo: Chuo Koronsha.

Fukui, Haruhiro. Jiyuminshutō to seisaku-kettei [The Liberal Democratic Party and policy making]. Tokyo: Fukumura Shuppan, 1969.

Henshubu (editorial staff). "Komeito no taishitsu to kino" [Character and functions of komeito]. Asahi janaru, March 5, 1967.

Higuchi, Kinichi. "Senkyo, Seitō, habatsu" [Elections, political parties and factions]. Dōshisha hōgaku [Doshisha law review] 12 (1961): 41-71.

Ishida, Takeshi. Gendai soshiki-ron [Contemporary organization theory]. Tokyo: Iwanami Shoten, 1961.

_____. Nihon no seiji Bunka [Japan's political culture]. Tokyo: Tokyo Daigaku Shuppan-Kai, 1970.

Jichisho senkyobu (Election Bureau, Ministry of Local Autonomy). Shugiin giin sosenkyo kekkashirabe [Results of general elections for the House of Representatives]. Tokyo: Election Bureau, Ministry of Local Autonomy, 1970.

_____. Toitsu chihosenkyo kekkashirabe [Results of unified local elections]. Tokyo: Election Bureau, Ministry of Local Autonomy, 1951-73.

Jinji Koshinjo. Jinji Koshin roku [Who's who]. Tokyo: Jinji Koshinjo, 1903- .

Jiyu (Liberty). A monthly magazine. Tokyo.

Jiyuminshuto (Liberal Democratic Party). Soshiki chōsakai tōshin [Report of the Organization Investigation Commission]. Tokyo: Jiyuminshuto, January 1963.

Kanagawa-ken, kikaku chōsabu tokeichōsaka (Statistics Survey Section, Planning and Research Department, Kanagawa Prefecture), ed. Kensei yōran [Prefectural Census Survey]. Yokohama: Kanagawa-ken, 1969 and 1972.

Kawakami, Tamio. "Habatsu rikigaku ni tsuiteno ichi Kōsatsu" [The mechanism of factions in Japanese political parties: an analysis]. Kōdōkagaku Kenkyu [Behavioral science research] 2 (1966): 29-36.

Keizai hyoron [Economic critique]. A monthly magazine. Tokyo.

Kikuoka, Yaozo, ed. Kokkai benran [Diet handbook]. Tokyo: Nihon Seikei Shimbun Shuppanbu, 1955-75.

Komei senkyo renmei (Clean Election Federation).

Kyoikushimbunsha, ed. Nikon kyoiku nenkan [Japan Education yearbook]. Tokyo: Kyoikushimbunsha, 1971.

Mainichi Shimbun [Mainichi newspaper]. Tokyo.

Masumi, Junnosuke. "Jiyuminshutō no soshiki to kinō [Organization and functions of the Liberal Democratic Party]. In Gendai nihon no seitō to kanryō [The parties and bureaucracy in contemporary Japan], edited by Nihon seiji-gakkai (Japanese Political Science Association), pp. 34-77. Tokyo: Iwanami Shoten, 1967.

_____. Nihon seitoshi-ron [A history of Japanese political parties]. Vols. 1-4. Tokyo: Tokyo University Press, 1965-68.

Naimusho chihokyoku (Local Bureau, Ministry of Home Affairs). Showa 22 nen 4 gatsu shikko shugiingiin, sangiingiin, todofuken-chiji, shikuchoson-cho, chihōgikaigiin sōsenkyo kekkashirabe [Results of general elections for the House of Representatives, House of Councillors, Prefectural Governors, City, Ward, Town and Village Mayors and Local Assemblies held in April 1947]. Tokyo: Ministry of Home Affairs, 1947.

Nakano, Tatsuo, and Shigetaro Iizuka. Shakaitō-Minshatō [The Japan Socialist Party and the Democratic Socialist Party]. Tokyo: Sekkasha, 1968.

Nara, Moryoshi. Tokyo tomin no tohyokōdō kara mita seitō shijiso no bunseki [Analysis of voting behavior in Tokyo areas]. Tokyo: Minshushugi Kenkyu-kai, 1966.

Nihon no Ugoki [The movement in Japan]. A monthly magazine.

Nihon seiji-gakkai (Japanese Political Science Association), ed. Gendai nihon no seitō to kanryō [The parties and bureaucracy in contemporary Japan]. Tokyo: Iwanami Shoten, 1967.

Nihon sogo kenkyujo, ed. Jyumin-sanka ni kansuru kenkyo. Tokyo: Shiryo-hen, 1976.

Nisihira, Sigeki. "Senkyo kara mita kakuto no genjyo to shorai" [The present situation and the future of each party viewed from the general elections]. Tenbo (April 1967): 57.

Nishijima, Hisashi. Komeitō [Clean Government Party]. Tokyo: Sekkasha, 1968.

Okabe, Keizo, and Joji Watanuki. Kokusai ishiki chōsa [International Political Consciousness Survey]. Tokyo: 1968. Mimeographed.

Okamura, Tadao. "Gendai nihon ni okeru seijiteki shakaika" [Political socialization in contemporary Japan]. In Gendai nihon ni okeru seijitaido no keisei to kōzō [Formation and structure of political attitudes in contemporary Japan], edited by Nihon seiji-gakkai (Japanese Political Science Association). Tokyo: Iwanami Shoten, 1971.

Ōkurashō insatsukyoku (Printing Bureau, Ministry of Finance). Shokuin-roku [Official register]. Tokyo: Okurasho Insatsukyoku, 1972.

Ori, Kan. "Amerikagashukoku ni okeru gunkenjishoku no seijiteki seikaku ni kansuru ichi kōsatsu" [American politics and the prosectorial office]. Amerika kenkyu [The American review] 7 (1973): 145-68.

Rodosho (Ministry of Labor). Rodo tokei nenkan [Labor statistical yearbook]. Tokyo: Rodosho, 1973.

Sangiin jimukyoku (House of Councillors Secretariat). Sangiin giin senkyo ichiran [House of Councillors elections]. Tokyo: House of Councillors Secretariat, 1965.

_____. Sangiin yoran [House of Councillors Survey]. Tokyo: Sangiin Jimukyoku, 1956-74.

Scalapino, Robert A., and Junnosuke Masumi. Gendai nihon no seitō to seiji [Parties and politics for contemporary Japan]. Tokyo: Iwanami Shoten, 1962.

Sekai [World]. A monthly magazine. Tokyo.

Shimane-ken (Shimane Prefecture). Kensei yōran [Prefectural Census Survey]. Matsue, Shimane: Shimanesken tokei kyokai, 1972.

Shinohara, Hajime, and Yonosuke Nagai, eds. "Seiji katci ni okeru shudanka" [The trend toward groups formation in the political process]. In Gendai seijigaku nyumon [An introduction to contemporary political science], edited by Hajime Shinohara and Yonosuke Nagai. Tokyo: Yuhikaku, 1965.

Shiso [Thoughts]. A monthly magazine. Tokyo.

Shugiin jimukyoku (House of Representatives Secretariat). Shugiin giin sosenkyo ichiran [A report on the general elections for the House of Representatives]. Tokyo: House of Representatives Secretariat, 1948-73.

_____. Shugiin yōran [House of Representatives Survey]. Tokyo: Shugiin Jimukyoku: House of Representatives Secretariat, 1955-73.

Soma, Masao. Nihon no senkyo [Japanese elections]. Tokyo: Ushio Shuppansha, 1967.

Sōrifu tōkeikyoku (Bureau of Statistics, Office of the Prime Minister). Jyumintōroku jinkoido hōkoku nenpo [Annual report of population movement from the Residence Registry]. Tokyo: Nihon Tōkei Kyokai, 1950-72.

_____. Kokusei chōsa hōkoku [National Census report]. Tokyo: Nihon Tōkei Kyokai, 1950-72.

_____. Nihon tōkei nenkan [Japan statistical yearbook]. Tokyo: Nihon Tōkei Kyokai, 1950-72.

Thayer, N. B. Jimintō [The Liberal Democratic Party]. Translated by Kobaysahi Katsumi. Tokyo: Sekkasha, 1968.

Tsuji, Kiyoaki. Nihon kanryōsei no kenkyu [A study of the Japanese bureaucracy]. Tokyo: Tokyo Daigaku Shuppankai, 1971.

Ushio [Tide]. A monthly magazine. Tokyo.

Watanabe, Tsuneo. Habatsu: hoshutō no kaibō [Factionalism: an analysis of the Conservative Party]. Tokyo: Kōbundō, 1958.

_____. Habatsu to tatōka jidai [Factionalism and an era of the multi-party trend]. Tokyo: Sekkasha, 1967.

_____. Tōshu to seitō [Party president and political parties]. Tokyo: Kōbundō, 1961.

Yomiuri, Shimbun, ed. Seitō: sono soshiki to habatsu no jittai [Political parties: their organizations and factional realities]. Tokyo: Yomiuri Shimbunsha, 1966.

Yoshimura, Tadashi. Nihon seiji no shindan [A diagnosis of Japanese politics]. Tokyo: Seishin Shobō, 1964.

INDEX

age of politics, 119
Almond and Verba, 81
attitudes toward koenkai (see Liberal Democratic Party)

Buchanan and Tullock, 82
bureaucracy, 12; influence on business, 40, 42; influence on parties, 39-40
business, support of LDP, 39-40, 42, 75

Cabinet, 17
coalition theory, 83-84
collective goods theory, 4, 83, 130-33, 135; centralization/ decentralization, 132; classes of goods, 131; demands on government, 133; economies/ diseconomies of scale, 131, 132; externalities, 5, 131, 133; free riders, 5; governmental size, 132; impact on factions, 81-82; impact on institutions, 130, 131-32; private goods, 131, 133; public goods, 131
community disintegration, 139
consensus decision making, 140
conservative bloc in Diet, 24, 28
Constitution, 17
convergence theory, 11
corporate model, corporatism, 2, 118
Cramer's Vs, 104-5
critical theory, 130, 133-35; capitalism, 133; hegemony, 131; imperialism, 133; language, 134; Marxism, 133,
134; multinational corporations, 133; positional goods, 135-36; state, role of, 134; system breakdown, 133-34; voting, 135; zero-sum goods, 135
cultural explanation theory, 11

decision making (ringeisei), 8, 140
decline of political parties, 6
demands on political parties, 138
Democratic Socialist Party, 24, 55, 102; Domei, 44, 75
Deutsch, 71, 73, 80
Diet, 15-16, 115, 139; electoral system, 18-19; factions, 67, 79-80, 83, 87
Domei, 44, 75

Eisenstadt, 11
electoral systems, 18-19; independent candidates, 19; minor parties, 18-19; voter participation, 19-20, 24
Emic/etic paradox, 8
endogenous models, 11, 33, 139, 140; impact on modernization, 11
entropy, impact on coalitions, 85-87; impact on LDP, 84
exogenous models, 11

factions (habatsu), 8, 35-38, 100, 118, 139; causes, 66, 68-69, 79-82; collective goods theory, 81; consequences, 66-67, 69; functions, 67; impact on Diet, 67, 80; impact of industrializa-

185

ABOUT THE AUTHORS

ROGER BENJAMIN is Professor of Political Science at the University of Minnesota, Minneapolis, Minnesota.

Professor Benjamin's research interests are in comparative politics, political economy, and comparative public policy. His recent work has appeared in the American Political Science Review, American Journal of Political Science, Journal of Conflict Resolution, Comparative Political Studies, Law and Society Review, Journal of Asian Studies, Journal of Peace Science, Social Science Quarterly, and numerous edited volumes. His most recent book is The Limits of Politics: Collective Goods and Political Change in Postindustrial Societies (Chicago: University of Chicago Press, 1980).

Professor Benjamin holds a B.A. from Michigan State University, East Lansing, Michigan, and his Ph.D. from Washington University, St. Louis, Missouri.

KAN ORI is Professor of Political Science at the Institute of International Relations, Sophia University, Tokyo.

Professor Ori's research interests are in comparative, American, and Japanese politics. His work has appeared in Quality & Quantity (The European-American Journal of Methodology), Journal of International Studies, Cybernetics and Society, Annual Review of the Japanese Political Science Association, International Relations (of the Japanese Association of International Relations), and numerous other Japanese and English language edited volumes.

Professor Ori holds a B.A. from Taylor University, Upland, Indiana, and his Ph.D. from Indiana University, Bloomington, Indiana.